YOU AND YOUR MUSE

CULTIVATE A JOURNEY OF STORYTELLING

KATE JOHNSTON

Ryebird Books

You and Your Muse: cultivate a journey of storytelling

First Edition (2025)

Copyright © Kate Johnston (2025).

ISBN: 979-8-9920769-0-5

Published by Ryebird Books

Cover Design by Tom Holbrook

Editing by Alison Huff, Dark Star Lit

Printed in the United States of America

CONTENTS

Introduction   1

Part One

Discover Your Muse   7

1. You Are A Writer If You Write   11

2. The Discovery Stage   17

3. Journaling   27

4. Daily Rituals For Creative Development   31

5. Natural Writing Forces   41

6. Creativity, Every Day   47

7. Finding Your Writing Process   53

Part Two

Write With Your Muse   61

8. Getting To Know Your Story   65

9. Where To Begin   69

10. Story Structure   83

11. Plot   99

12. Protagonist + Antagonist   107

13. Theme   115

14. The Goal And The Lesson   123

15. The Ghost And Flawed Belief   129

16. Weaknesses   135

17. Motivation Drives Action   143

18. Character Building   149

19. Using Inner Conflict To Drive Your Story   155

20. Using External Conflict To Drive Your Story   161

21. Scene Building   167

22. Setting   179

23. Showing Versus Telling   191

24. Art Of Suspense   201

25. Tone & Mood   209

26. Voice & Style   217

Part Three

Journey With Your Muse   225

27. Your Purpose   229

28. Bust Through Writer's Block   237

29. Revising Draft 0   247

30. The Inner Critic   257

31. Seasons Of Stagnation   263

32. Mapping Out Your Writing Journey   269

33. Believe In Your Audacious Dream   279

Acknowledgements   289

References   293

Author's Note   295

About The Author   297

INTRODUCTION

Writing, for me, is as natural as breathing. This is both a gift and a curse, however, because with this blessing comes the expectation that it should be easy.

Writing may be a natural part of my life, but it has never been easy.

I've lost count of how many stories I've written, rewritten, discarded, printed out, lost to cyber gremlins, shelved, burned; submitted to writing instructors, contests, literary agents, small publishers, writing groups, editors, coaches; shared with family members, friends, frenemies.

I've lost track of the number of wishes and dreams I've held in my heart, how many times I sealed an envelope addressed to an agent (back in the day when we mailed submission packages through the post office—just to give you an idea of how long I've really been at this gig) or pressed the SEND button on my computer, thinking, This is it, this is the one that'll make it.

I've come close dozens of times, but that's not enough in this business. For someone who breathes creativity, "close" feels more like unworthiness.

For a long time, "Why is it so hard for me?" was a daily question. While such low moments are painful, they can also be transformative. I've suffered through my fair share of Dark Nights of the Soul, and I've always come through learning something new about myself and my creative life, feeling ready to try again.

In my search for creative success, I've been told that I'm inspiring and motivating to other writers. Go figure. Maybe it's because I see myself in their struggles, their shattered wishing-stars, the labyrinth their writing journey has become.

Thankfully, I recognized my coaching and mentoring abilities in time to build a freelance business supporting emerging and experienced writers of all genres. Over the years—while juggling a family, personal responsibilities, my fumbling fiction writing—I turned all my failures and disappointments into lessons and "teaching moments" for other writers. I created courses and workshops, wrote handbooks, blogged and newsletter-ed and video-ed.

Some of my content was great; some of it stank. When a course or a book didn't fare well, panic would set in. That feeling of unworthiness would trickle back into my brain, taunting me that I'm on track to fail again. Another Dark Night of the Soul would loom, cackling.

However, because writing must be embedded into my DNA, I push through. I don't always know how I overcome those periods of intense fear, where I encounter the dreaded thought that my creativity has abandoned me for real this time, just that I manage to eventually emerge into the light.

And try again.

As these cycles of creative gains and losses became relatively common, I began to learn how to countermove. It proved to be an interesting period of growth for me. My passion for writing was always the catalyst. I could have given up and gone into sales or something equally life-threatening, but my determination is proof of how deeply ingrained the desire to write is within me.

At the center of all of this is the relationship that I nurtured with my creativity. When I began to treat it as a living, breathing part of me, something sparked.

My creativity became my Muse.

And this relationship took off! It no longer mattered if I was going to make my Audacious Dreams come true, only that I enjoyed the ride. That I learned how to separate my sense of worthiness from the ups and downs of a business that isn't in my control. That I stopped identifying with my limiting beliefs and started identifying with my Muse.

It only mattered that I honored my Muse by showing up.

My Muse. There is no other Muse like it in the whole world. And the same is true for you. Everyone has a Muse, whether they see themselves as creative or not, so it's up to you to decide what kind of relationship you cultivate with it.

That's what I intend with this book—to help writers cultivate a relationship with their own personal Muse so that they can forge a writing journey that brings them joy, fulfillment, and growth.

Whether you're someone who wants to write but doesn't know how to start; someone who doesn't know if they'll enjoy writing; someone who used to enjoy writing; someone who is struggling with inspiration, motivation, or momentum; someone who told themselves they'd like to write but think they'll be bad at it . . .

Basically, if you're someone who has felt the magical energy between fingers and keyboard, or pen and paper . . .

This book is for you.

I've structured the book into three parts. The first, Discover Your Muse, teaches you ways to cultivate a strong and dependable relationship with your Muse so that you can begin (or continue) a writing journey that lights you up. This includes identifying the conditions under which you work best, exploring strategies to get started, and developing a writing practice that encourages growth and aligns with your goals.

Write with Your Muse is part two, and this section is filled with lessons on the fundamentals of fiction writing, including pointers on developing your protagonist, how to build a scene, and when to use showing versus telling. This guidance can be treated as a refresher for writers who are familiar with the basics, or for those emerging writers, as an introduction to story development.

Forging a writing journey alongside your real-world life is a thrilling but daunting prospect. Part three of this book, Journey with Your Muse, teaches strategies to sustain a healthy relationship with your Muse, putting your learned skills and knowledge to work for you in the face of Life's surprises and challenges, and adopting an empowered belief system. Whether you're someone who struggles to finish a draft or lacks the belief that you're a good-enough writer, these final chapters can offer encouragement, advice, and clarity.

A list of discovery questions follows each chapter to help you roll out your story and your journey as a writer.

Treat this book as a resource, a tool, a comrade-in-arms, a friend. Allow yourself to become a part of the inspiration and motivation within. Find the words that light you up, and let them carry you into the netherworld of creativity. Here, in these pages, you'll be shown just how worthy you and your writing dreams are.

PART ONE

DISCOVER YOUR MUSE

DISCOVER YOUR MUSE

Muse

/myooz/

: any of the nine sister goddesses in Greek mythology presiding over song and poetry and the arts and sciences

: a source of inspiration

—from Merriam-Webster

In this book, I often refer to the source of a writer's creativity as their Muse. I see this source of creativity as a natural part of everyone (writers and nonwriters alike), but not everyone necessarily taps into it, or if they do, it isn't always in a way that serves them.

You and your Muse need to learn how to co-create so that you can be successful in your writing journey. Every Muse operates in its own special way—do you know how your Muse operates? Are you honoring the work it does? Do you know when it's sending you ideas to strengthen your main character or pointing out a plot hole? Have you developed a writing practice so that when you're ready to write, your Muse is ready to rock-and-roll, too?

This kind of relationship takes time and effort to develop, and many writers neglect this work. They just want to write their books, but then they wonder why they keep getting pummeled by distractions, or why they're constantly slamming into writer's blocks, or why they can't finish a draft.

Even if there's something flawed in the story, the reason such writers often struggle to fix the problem or seem to have the same difficulties running on replay is because they're not in tune with their Muse.

Over the next few chapters, I'll offer suggestions and strategies to help you build a relationship with your Muse so that you can begin, develop, and finish your stories.

I highly suggest doing this work as part of a prewriting strategy because it will strengthen your position as a writer preparing for their next project. You'll also learn interesting traits about who you are as a person embarking upon (or continuing) a writing journey—traits that support you or hinder you. This information will aid your overall productivity and creativity, so you'll not only be better equipped to reach your personal finish line, but you'll grow and evolve along the way.

Ready to discover your Muse? Let's hop to it.

1

Mapping Out Your Writing Journey

You are a writer.

Did you need to hear that?

You are a writer.

Yeah, yeah, I know that I don't know you, so making this claim is pretty ballsy, but only a writer is going to pick up this book and start flipping through the pages. And writers sometimes need to be told by a stranger that yes, indeed, they are writers. Hearing it from their mom, significant other, or their cat doesn't always do the trick. Not when the plot is going sideways, or when a two-star review pops up, or when a blank page is blinking madly from the computer, or when a submission gets rejected. Again.

Not when they've yet to be published.

Not when they haven't finished a story.

Not when they're only writing for a couple of hours here and there.

So, I want to let you in on a little secret. A writer's identity has nothing to do with the quality of the writing, how long they've been writing, or if they've sent seventy-seven queries without a bite.

A writer is a writer because they write.

I'm bringing this up because I want to get it out in the open and out of the way. Throughout this book, we'll be roaming through elements of storytelling and how to engage with your Muse—and it's just all-around helpful if you understand and accept, right now, that you are a writer.

Okay, so now that we're on the same page, I want to make you aware of some mind-gremlins that like to mess with you and your identity as a writer.

COMPARISONITIS

Writers tend to seek external validation because that's the most obvious evidence they can cite to prove their writer-worthiness. But when writers do that, they're opening themselves up to judgments and opinions from anyone who has a judgment or an opinion to give. As one can imagine, that gets messy. Fast.

Appreciation for writing, for storytelling, is subjective. What one person may praise, another may jeer. If a writer is seeking feedback or validation from someone who isn't their "ideal reader," then that writer is setting themselves up for painful disappointment.

Negative comments can be enough to torpedo a writer's confidence. They might compare themselves to other writers and measure their progress based on someone else's success. Self-critical thoughts rush in, such as, "I must be a terrible writer because I haven't been published yet, but that writer has, and she's only been writing for two months!" They question if they're good enough, if they're talented enough, if they have thick-enough skin, and gosh darn it, if people even like them.

This comparison game can lead writers to their doom.

First and foremost: The writing world is big enough for all of us. Second: Each of us has our own path to forge in this world. Any time you feel the urge to compare yourself to another writer, ask yourself how much you know about their background, their family history, their writing experiences, their goals for their writing journey, the gremlins that prey upon them . . . I promise you'll end up with a lot of unanswered questions. We don't know what struggles another writer has endured before achieving their wins. Let's celebrate their victories and use them as proof that success and fortune are available to us all.

IMPOSTER SYNDROME

Maya Angelou, an award-winning writer and poet, suffered doubts about her accomplishments. "I've run a game on everybody, and they're going to find me out."

Despite the fact that we term this feeling of fraudulence as a "syndrome," it's important to understand that it's not a disease or abnormality. People from all walks of life, irrespective of age, race, socioeconomic status, educational attainment, or gender, often grapple with feelings of undeservingness regarding the positive attention they get for their work. In fact, according to a journal article published by the National Library of Medicine, studies evaluated the prevalence rates of imposter syndrome and found up to 82 percent of people feel incompetent and unable to accept credit for their accomplishments.

Imposter syndrome tends to strike us when we're on a winning streak, when everything seems to be falling into place. And despite how hard we've worked to earn these wins, we may still feel like we don't deserve them.

Of course, this is just a fear-driven gremlin wreaking havoc in our heads.

Talking about this sense of fraudulence openly can help ease the burden of feeling like a phony among genuine peers. Personally, I have yet to meet a single accomplished writer who has never struggled with imposter syndrome or something similar. Knowing we're not alone makes us feel stronger and more capable of continuing onward. When we band together, that gremlin doesn't stand a chance against us.

FEAR OF (FILL IN THE BLANK)

The fear gremlin covers a whole slew of bases. Fear can cause us to procrastinate, to avoid finding time to write, to succumb to "shiny object syndrome" and frequently switch writing projects, to not finish our projects, to be resistant to constructive feedback, to revise the same chapters repeatedly, to give into distractions, to melt down at rejections, and many, many more hurdles.

However, fear can also be helpful. It might be telling you that you're onto something that matters greatly. Fear may be letting you know that you're about to step outside your comfort zone, so you better look alive. Fear can show you that you're about to do some major growth work—that your life is leveling up.

Treating fear as a herald—rather than a threat—can really work wonders. This means you have to get comfortable taking risks, putting yourself out there, and trying new things, but that all naturally leads to growth and expansion.

The act of writing is enough to qualify someone as a writer, but it's a basic starting point. There will come a time in your journey when other aspects play a role, such as skill-building, application of story principles, and publication goals. Usually, the more intentional we are, the more the gremlins want to come and play games in our heads. Just remember, they're showing up because you're taking a chance on yourself, not because you're somewhere you don't belong.

As you forge ahead and learn more about how to write stories, you'll also discover more about who you are as a writer. This includes getting to know your Muse and what makes that source of your inspiration flourish. Some of your habits, motivations, traits, values, goals, action steps, moods, and beliefs will serve you well. Some will work against you. Others, you'll have to cultivate from scratch, depending on what you need or want in your journey. Keep notes. Try new ways of doing things. Be open-minded and flexible.

With time, practice, and ferocity, you and your Muse can co-create a productive and fulfilling writing journey.

DISCOVERY WORK

Research some of your favorite authors. If they have a blog, read as many posts as you can. Check out any interviews they may have done. Pay careful attention to what that author says about fear or any other mind-gremlin they may have experienced. They may even offer up a mindset hack that could help you.

Pull any and all quotes you can find and post them in your writing habitat. Use these quotes to remind you that all writers wrestle with low confidence, discouragement, and fear. It's just part of the gig, and you're not alone.

2

THE DISCOVERY STAGE

Getting started can be one of the biggest hurdles for writers to overcome. For beginners, the difficulty may result from having no clue about what to focus on first, or they may be unsure whether they're "doing it the right way." More experienced writers may seize up at the notion of launching into a new project because they're still reeling from the last one, or maybe doubt is taking its toll because writing a book is hard work.

Even though every writer has their own way of doing things, I think it's safe to say that all of them go through some version of discovery before they begin the actual drafting process.

Discovery is also known as brainstorming. Some writers "discover" their story while doing the dishes and daydreaming, researching in the wee hours of the night, sketching out character arcs, or outlining the plot. How and when a writer does their discovery work depends on their personal preferences. There is no one way, and there is no wrong way.

I'm going to assume that, because you're reading this book, you're curious about the writing life—and maybe you're even toying with a story idea on some level. It may be a seed that you haven't yet tried to develop through written words. The story idea might revolve around a single image, or it may be multilayered. Perhaps your idea was inspired by a memory of a wedding gone wrong or rumors of underground tunnels in your hometown. Your idea could be something you imagined and developed over years, or it might be something that struck out of the blue.

I want to express clearly that, no matter where you are in your journey, **all** story ideas have potential. And this means that **all** writers have potential.

There may be circumstances where an idea feels troublesome. This might lead you to think it's a crummy idea, or worse—make you doubt your ability.

The trick with any idea is to first accept it as being possible to develop, and second, to test it out to see if it's a good fit for you now—and that's what you can do in the discovery stage. Not only that, but you can also strengthen your relationship with your Muse and shape the kind of journey you want to follow—all before the actual hardcore writing begins.

Even though all story ideas have potential, they require hard work and sacrifice to develop into a concept. For writers who aren't mentally and soulfully prepared for the uphill battle that is writing a story, the grind can be disillusioning.

Some ideas will take more time and effort compared to others, and you may find that you lose interest in certain ones for reasons unknown. Even with all the energy and passion that go into spinning our ideas into full-blown stories, we're never guaranteed to take them all the way to the finish line.

It's entirely possible that a story you thought you wanted to share with readers turns out to be more for your creative growth or mental health instead. Sometimes, a story ends up in a drawer or under the bed, even after wrangling it for months or years. The work can be so draining that it fizzles out the magic spell between a writer and a story—or, even more discouragingly, between a writer and their Muse.

I'm not bringing this up to scare you off! On the contrary. I mention these pitfalls so that you can be a well-armed writer as you move forward in your journey. Too often, writers get so tangled up in setbacks and overwhelm, disappointments and detours, obstacles and landslides, that we lose sight of what's really important.

Our growth.

Treating a defeat, rejection, or stumble as a reflection of your writing ability—or worse, your self-worth—will have you chasing your own tail (while simultaneously spiraling downward). Sure, having a destination in mind is helpful to set goals and steer ourselves accordingly, but if we value the outcome more than our growth (a.k.a. learning) along the way, we will burn out, drain out, and all-around tap out.

While making mistakes is a vital part of the human experience and growth, we can lose our way if we let our mistakes and poor choices define us. Be clear on your destination, but nurture your journey and treat the rough patches as opportunities to learn, pivot, and try again.

The discovery stage is not just a time for you to get to know your story. It's a critical time for you to get to know yourself as a writer. Take advantage of the early days of your journey to cultivate your relationship with your Muse and to build your confidence as a writer.

CURIOSITY AND EXPLORATION

To engage with their Muse, a writer has to be curious and willing to explore the unknown. These two key components can help a writer to get started and guide them through the discovery stage.

Writers must want to know *why* and *how come* and *when* and *what does that mean* and *how could something like that possibly happen* and *what is going to happen next?*

But writers don't stop there. They seek answers and explanations and information and solutions. They see a cause and want to figure out the effect. They stumble upon a mystery and want to hunt for clues. They get a hold of information and they ask, "So what?" They hear a conversation and listen for emotion. Writers feel their way through the world by following the telltale signs of a story.

As you become more comfortable engaging with your Muse, look for the unexpected. Look for something that's a little bit out of the ordinary. Something that tilts left when everything else goes right. Something that smolders, something that sparkles.

Stories launch from a point where something unusual or out of the ordinary happens. In literary terms, this is called the Inciting Incident—it's the game-changing moment that puts your character on the path of the main conflict. Without this unexpected event, the rest of the story can't take place.

Part of your exploration involves searching for an Inciting Incident that can launch a whole story. Once you come upon something that feels right enough to be unusual, dig around this moment—asking *Why? Why not? What if? What's happening here? So what?*—those are some of the most important questions in a writer's toolkit that need to be answered.

Those questions allow you to develop a story that showcases a protagonist with a problem that needs to be solved, but something or someone is in their way. As they become more mired in their attempts to reach their goal, the stakes and consequences loom and escalate, and they're forced to deal not just with external opposition but internal opposition. The plot unravels at a compelling pace, and the protagonist's growing awareness of (and desire to combat) their inner demons stirs reader empathy. These elements and design principles must work together to pull the reader through the story's labyrinth, so they begin to feel that it all *means something*. The story becomes a vicarious experience for the reader. They're invested on a personal level, and they must see it through to the end.

No small feat.

However, the early stages of writing can feel overwhelming when you're worrying about how to pull a whole story together. Be aware of design principles, yes. Be clear on your ultimate job as a writer, yes. But when you're in the discovery stage of your story, it's more important to have an open and trusted line of communication with your Muse. Your confidence as a writer will help you reach your personal finish line.

If you feel like you work better with deadlines or some kind of structure, then you should set your own time limits and framework. Be mindful that this period of relationship-building and idea-developing can take time. Be patient and flexible and willing to try new ways of doing things. Figure out what works best for you, as everyone has their own set of conditions under which they thrive.

In my chapter on natural writing forces, I talk more about the importance of knowing who you are as a writer and under what conditions you perform best, both of which will empower you to make efficient progress along your writing journey.

As you proceed, keep checking your "creative temperature." Using a range of one to ten—with ten+ being LIGHTS ME UP and one being I'D RATHER DEEP-CLEAN THE BATHROOM—determine what this story means to you. A story worth writing is one that makes you want to sit down and invest your heart, time, and energy (despite the fact you have teenage boys and the bathroom is in serious need of a deep clean). If you're losing interest, getting distracted, coming up with excuses for why you can't "find the time" to write, then that story may not be the right fit for you right now. Simply put it aside for the time being and work on something else. You can always come back to it another day.

It's important to note that there is a difference between writing a story for yourself and writing a story for an audience. A story for yourself can (and often will) read indulgently, whereas a story for others needs to follow certain guidelines and design principles (as mentioned previously). You may want to write the story for yourself first and then revise it to meet the standards of an audience, and this can be an especially helpful approach for beginner writers.

As your idea grows, you'll want to test it along the way. Now, I know I said that all ideas have potential—and they do! But some ideas are better as personal essays, where others are more suited for a short-story collection or a novella. Then, there are those ideas that are merely practice runs, the stories that we lovingly craft but can't quite seem to get into shape for an audience beyond ourselves, our moms, or our cats.

FROM IDEA TO CONCEPT

Writers can feel excited about a story idea, but an idea—on its own—isn't enough to carry the weight of a story. They need to turn their idea into a story concept. The main difference between an idea and a concept is specificity. Where an idea is abstract, a concept is concrete. An idea needs to be developed with specific events and details to start feeling like a story with a beginning, middle, and end.

A story concept has the power to engage a reader's interest because it showcases a compelling main character whose pursuit of a goal against all odds impacts them on a deeper level, forcing them to grow and transform internally as a result.

Story Idea: I want to write a story about a fish that gets lost in the ocean.

Story Concept: I want to write a story about a clownfish struggling for independence from his overprotective father who accidentally gets captured by a fishing boat and must learn how to take care of himself until he can find a way to get back home. (*Finding Nemo*)

Basically, your idea is auditioning for a particular role, and you have to be clear on what that role is. An epic space opera? Short story about a family? Contemporary love story? Blog post series on homesteading? Harry Potter fan fiction? When you have a clear enough idea of what you're writing, you can begin testing it to see what you have in place, what's missing, and what you need to continue developing.

Some ideas have the natural juice needed to evolve into a concept, while others need a bit of pulverizing to get to the juice. One of the best ways to do it is to keep asking those simple, but important, questions:

- So what?

- What's happening here?

- What if?

- Why?

- Why not?

- How can things get worse?

Answer those questions fully and confidently as you develop your rough draft (or outline), and you'll have a marvelous story in the palm of your hands. And if you can't quite nail down the answers right now, don't fret. It doesn't necessarily mean the story has no inherent juice, and it definitely doesn't mean you aren't a good-enough writer. It could need more time to cook, or a dozen other reasons could be at play.

This is why honoring and nurturing the journey is so important. If you start beating yourself up if the story isn't quite working, you lose out on a learning opportunity. Instead, let it be part of your writer's growth. Treat it as a gateway to practice skills or build confidence that will serve you in another storytelling endeavor.

DISCOVERY WORK

1.| Test one of your story ideas with the following questions:
   Why?
   Why not?
   What will happen next?
   How can things get worse?
   What if?

2.| Try developing your story idea into a basic story concept using this simple formula:
   [Main character] wants to [do something that matters greatly to them], but [obstacle].

3.| Test your story's stakes by answering this question:
   Who is fighting against whom, for what, and why?

3

JOURNALING

I am a big believer in regular, if not daily, journaling. However, out of all the suggestions I give to writers, journaling is the one that gets the most pushback. I think people tend to misinterpret how a journal can be used. They automatically equate the exercise with writing about their day or the inner workings of their minds. While journaling is great for that, I use mine to help build and sustain my writing practice.

Journaling is a written record, so it can help you monitor your writing progress—from your daily word counts to your short- and long-term goals. You can use your journal to work out problems in your story or to jot down ideas that hit you when you're not in your writing session. Depending on how many reasons you journal, you can use different journals for different components of your writing practice.

You can also monitor how you're feeling about your writing—basically doing a creative health check-up. These appointments with yourself can be done daily, weekly, monthly, or anytime you feel like you need to sort things out with your Muse.

Journaling provides a timeline of your writing history, the ups and downs, the wins and setbacks, lessons learned and tips to remember. This, in turn, gives you valuable insight about yourself as a writer, your process, your goals, and anything else that impacts your writing life.

I have several different journals going at any given time. I use the traditional hardbound journals, and I keep them scattered around the house—there's even one in my car. This is simply because my mind is usually wheeling through story ideas—like chasing butterflies—so I catch them on paper, holding them still, until I can sit down for my next writing session and properly deal with them.

However, there are "seasons" when creativity is elusive. This can happen for any number of reasons. I use my journal to "talk" myself through these darker periods, and because I've been recording them for years, I have a history of those ups and downs in my creative life. Flipping through the pages is an eye-opening experience—common threads and triggers emerge, explaining why I'm at a low point. Anytime I'm struggling, I can look back and see how I pivoted toward a better direction in the past and use those same tricks.

Without that written record, it'd be too easy to keep sinking and beating myself up senselessly. Journaling has empowered my creative life, enabling me to connect more deeply to my Muse, to understand how I operate under certain conditions, and to learn how to overcome my flaws and harness my strengths.

DISCOVERY WORK

1.| Play around with different ways to journal.It's important to find a modality that you're more likely to use on a regular basis over the long term. I recommend dating all entries as a journal is a written record, and it helps to see what situations you're encountering at certain points in your life.

2.| Anytime you're feeling low or wobbly, write a supportive letter to yourself in your journal. When you find your way through the darkness, write about that too. These are your records, and they'll come in handy in the future.

3.| Stuck on something in your story? Journal it out! Sometimes, journaling through writing prompts can get us into a marvelous writer's mindset because we're writing expectation-free.

Here are some to get you started:

Lately, my character has been feeling . . . because . . .
This person/situation is making my character feel . . .
What past event/emotion is being triggered for my character?
Does my character fall into a pattern, and if so, how is it affecting them?
My character laughed about . . .

When my character visits . . . they feel . . .

Last night at the cocktail party, my character spotted . . . and this happened . . .

My character woke up from a nightmare, and it made her fear . . .

4

DAILY RITUALS FOR CREATIVE DEVELOPMENT

Bonding with your Muse is a surefire way to foster healthy creativity. I've found that rituals help me open the channels of communication with my Muse so that we can work together on a consistent basis.

I believe that regular practice is critical to building strong, lasting habits that will sustain you over the long term. To "practice" your writing, you don't need to dive neck-deep into a work-in-progress (WIP) every time you sit down to work. A writing practice can be made up of all kinds of tasks—character sketching, poetry, jotting down research notes, drawing maps of your story world, blog posts, discovery work. Even cleaning or organizing your writing habitat!

The key to a healthy, enjoyable, regular practice is a healthy, enjoyable, regular engagement with your Muse. There are days when I don't have the energy to even think about a WIP, much less crack open the computer file. But avoiding my Muse when I'm feeling wobbly about my creativity only invites more wobbles.

This is where rituals come in super-handy. I can engage in these rituals no matter how I'm feeling about my WIP or my creative ability and still nurture my relationship with my Muse. If, after the rituals, I don't feel like working on a story, there's no guilt because I logged time fostering creativity in other ways.

GRATITUDE & AFFIRMATIONS

Starting each day being thankful for what I already have takes my mind off the things I've yet to accomplish and allows me to appreciate the journey. Expressing gratitude in times of stress or angst calms and motivates me. I have struggled with bouts of anxiety and depression since I was a kid. It wasn't until I confided in my mom, when I was in my mid-thirties, that I learned about the so-called "family depression," a term coined by our cousin. I had the option to manage my mental health with medication, but because my bouts were short-lived and spiked randomly, long-term medication felt like overkill. I wanted to find a way to handle it naturally if I could.

That's when I stumbled upon spirituality. Not religion. Rather, nurturing a connection to a higher state of self-love, joy, and faith. Part of what helped me believe that spirituality was my way to go was how nature made me feel. When I sat among the trees or weeded my flower garden or listened to the songbirds or watched squirrels frolic, I was always overcome with a deep sense of peace and joy.

I'd heard about the mental health benefits of being outside, and when I learned that connecting to nature could be a way through the emotional and mental mess, I dug deeper.

What I love about practicing spirituality is that I can do it on my own terms. I don't have to adhere to a set of constricting rules, and I can focus on what is meaningful to me, personally.

One of my favorite spiritual tools is reciting affirmations. When I first started out, I used generic affirmations from spiritual leaders such as Gabby Bernstein and Shakti Gawain. As I grew more comfortable, I crafted my own affirmations that fit my specific situation. I'd set them as notifications on my phone so that they'd pop up randomly throughout the day. I also wrote them down on scraps of paper and tucked them in various places for me to stumble upon.

The following are a few that I use regularly:

"I attract the energy of creativity and feel it flow through me every day."

"My heart is open and ready to receive creativity in all its forms."

"I live each day in the beauty and bounty of creativity and have faith that I'm on the right path toward my dreams."

"I welcome an infinite stream of abundant creativity to flow through my life, and I channel it in productive, imaginative, and joyful ways."

Gratitude and affirmations led me down the super-fun path of creative visualization—including daydreaming, scripting, storytelling, and drawing—and that's where I really got into my spirituality practice. No surprise, seeing as how creative visualization allowed me to lean on my imagination to create what I wanted. Spend time using my imagination? Yes, please!

As I designed my own practice, I uncovered a lot of pieces from my past that I'd either forgotten or hidden or brushed off. I also gleaned a clearer understanding of my *self*, who I am in this world, and who I want to be. You might have heard how spirituality can lead to personal development, and this is why. An ongoing and consistent practice is eye-opening and soul-cleansing. Not only does it help you learn ways to cope with stress and other mental health issues, but it also helps you restore hope and optimism.

Having said that—I chose this route in lieu of therapy and medication. That may not necessarily be best for everyone. Some mental health conditions need professional treatment, so if you're unsure about your situation, please seek professional care to make an informed decision about your best next steps.

MAGIC SPELL

Before a writing session, I write down what I plan to accomplish for the session. This could include a specific story problem I want to tackle, research I need to conduct, a word count goal, or it could be a combination of several objectives. I also state why I want to focus on those particular tasks. I write it all out on a piece of paper and place it where I can see it in my workspace. This helps me stay accountable and gives me something concrete to shoot for.

In addition to writing down *what* and *why*, I add details about how I want to feel when I accomplish what I set out to do and what my next steps might look like.

For instance, if I want to start thinking about contacting beta readers, I might brainstorm what that will involve. All of this becomes a fairly detailed plan of action that helps me remain exceptionally clear on what I want to accomplish in the short and long term.

I call it a magic spell mainly to keep it fun and lighthearted, but also because, in a sense, that's what I'm conjuring. A spell is a bunch of ingredients that, when mixed together under the right conditions, will create something new that is useful in some way. By writing down my intentions and actions for my writing session, I'm conjuring a magic spell for a productive and creative one.

When I'm done with my spell, I clip it inside my journal to keep it as part of my record.

SECRET GARDEN OF WRITING

In the previous chapter, I talked about journaling. My secret garden of writing is different. This is where I let my creativity spill forth just for fun.

I have notebooks and traditional hardbound journals filled with pieces of writing, ideas, snippets of eavesdropped conversations, bad poetry, doodles, pretend words, and other sorts of creative ventures and musings that I share with no one else in the world.

This is my safe space, where I can roam, explore, and dare without fear of judgment or pressure.

My secret garden and my writing journals have some overlap, but for the most part, my secret garden is the place where I can freely express myself creatively without worrying about quality, beauty, or skill.

In a lot of ways, my secret garden of writing symbolizes a time in my life when writing was all fun—never scary or daunting. A time of pure innocence.

Nowadays, writing is more work than fun, more anxiety-inducing than pleasurable, more risky than joyful. (Yet, I'm still in it . . .)

The fact that my writing evolved into something that reflects a "coming of age" is somewhat discouraging because it means that somewhere along the line, I stopped writing for the innocence and joy of it. I have to consciously yank myself into a session of enthusiastic and pleasurable writing. That's where my secret garden of writing comes to the rescue—it reminds me of those easy days of playing pretend games with my sister, searching for wildlife in the woods, climbing trees, and reading late-late-late into the night.

JOURNALING

I won't say much here, as I already spent a chapter on it, but I want to reiterate that journaling is a solid ritual in my life that truly helps me stay on track with my writing practice. As I mentioned, I use traditional hardbound journals, but you don't have to. I have a client who uses spreadsheets for his journaling and another who uses an app on her phone. Use your favorite technique.

POWER HOUR

A ritual that helps keep me going in the middle of the day or when my energy begins to lag is what I call my Power Hour. I take a one-hour break to eat lunch and move my body. As a side gig, I walk dogs. Turns out, most dogs need a midday break too, so the timing works out nicely. Even if my day is dog-walk-free, I still take that hour to be physically active and remove myself from my study. No computer, no phone, no technology of any kind.

To be honest, this ritual was extremely difficult to implement. I tend to have working lunches and rarely take breaks because I immerse myself body-mind-soul in any project I have going. However, the decreased physical activity wreaked havoc on my body, so for health reasons, this ritual became a necessity. (This is also the reason I started walking dogs.)

When I return to the workday after my Power Hour, I'm more energized, more relaxed, more creative, and more focused. Admittedly, the first few minutes are tough, so I'll usually meditate on my magic spell of the day to remind myself what I want to accomplish, and that usually settles me back into my groove and the work zone.

RELAXING THE MIND AND THE BODY

My end-of-the-day ritual is a combination of journaling, yoga, and a book or meditation. I get off the computer and my phone at least one hour before bedtime. Or, if I'm watching television, I'll try to schedule my evening so the program ends within an hour of bedtime.

I'll take a few minutes to journal how my day went and what I'd like to get ready for the following day. I'm intentional about writing in the positive—even if something went kerflooey that day. The last thing I want to do at the end of any day is wallow in what didn't go well. I'll acknowledge it, because brushing it off isn't helpful in the long run, and depending on the situation, I might try to do some problem-solving. Ultimately, I aim to frame the events of my day in a way that leaves me feeling encouraged, hopeful, or satisfied.

Then, I start winding down with about thirty minutes of relaxing yoga. I try to keep my thoughts in the moment, not on what transpired earlier in the day or what's looming in the future. Finally, I get ready for bed and then I read. It's got to be a real book, one that can be held in my hands with pages that I can touch. I'm a frequent flier with my local library, and it's rare when I don't have a stack of books on my bedside table.

Lights out, and I'm usually calm and chill enough to fall asleep quickly. But there are those nights when my mind is nonstop. I have found a three-part meditation technique that works fairly well to counteract the frenetic loops in my head.

1.| I focus on slow, deep breaths. Often, I'll place a hand on my stomach so I can feel the breaths more deeply.

2.| I repeat a simple, positive phrase in my mind, such as "I am relaxed" or "All is well" or anything that feels comforting in the moment.

3.| I visualize a waterfall, a meadow of flowers, a forest, or any other kind of natural setting.

Occupying the mind through repetition of positive phrases and visualization of peaceful images while calming the body through breathwork can be very helpful in moments of stress, sleeplessness, or overwhelm. This technique is a form of meditation—with the objective of falling asleep—but it can be difficult to harness. Practice helps.

Rituals are sacred to me, not just for boosting my creative and mental health but also for keeping me on task from day to day, especially when the going gets tough.

The practice of setting a personal goal for yourself and then reflecting on the outcome will get you in the habit of taking yourself seriously and being clear about your intentions. Writing may be easy, but writing consistently over the long term—while growing and strengthening your skills—can be difficult. That's where forging a positive and supportive relationship with your Muse plays a big role—and it all starts with your intention.

DISCOVERY WORK

Want to give a ritual a shot? Try this as a pre-writing session ritual:

1.| Light a candle or incense. Play some instrumental background music. (I personally love soundtracks from films, television, and video games.)

2.| Get comfortable in a favorite spot and write down your daily writing goal in a special notebook or journal. (This will be your version of a magic spell, so craft it in whatever way feels good to you.)

3.| Next, recite a positive affirmation or prayer that seals the deal regarding your writing goal. Bonus points for writing it down on a piece of paper and posting it someplace where you can see it easily.

4.| After your writing session, return to the page where you wrote your goal and record your outcome. Reflect on this outcome and how it makes you feel. Be sure to congratulate yourself for accomplishing your goal (or, if you didn't fully accomplish it, honor yourself for showing up). Think about what you'd like to do for your next writing session and write down that intention.

5

Natural Writing Forces

Once upon a time, when the writing wasn't going so well, I explored my strengths, flaws, beliefs, workspace, time of day I chose to write, habits, personality traits, and values. These "natural writing forces"—labeled such because that's what they feel like to me—are natural parts of our lives that we have to learn how to manage for optimal productivity and creativity. Anything that seemed to impact my creativity was evaluated, critiqued, analyzed.

I learned a lot about who I was as a writer, how I held myself back, what external situations tended to block me, and what I needed to do to overcome these obstacles. Some of what I learned was obvious, and some of it was eye-opening.

At first, I was reluctant to make certain changes. However, as my struggles and disappointments continued, I finally decided to pivot. Drastically. Once I changed my ways and my outlook, a funny thing happened.

My writing life bloomed.

Despite the positive change, I still had to make conscious choices from one day to the next to ensure I stayed on the writing path. This meant a lot of self-observation and self-reflection, and taking action based on that information.

Journaling came in handy for that (surprise!). This fantastic mode of reflection and self-reporting helped me closely monitor my natural writing forces. When I recorded enough data, I was able to determine which internal and external forces impacted my writing. This made it possible to build a sustainable writing practice.

The tricky thing about natural writing forces is that they evolve with time and circumstance and growth, and they're made up of external factors (such as a 9–5 job or raising kids) and internal factors (such as moods or habits). Together, these things create an environment in which you'll either thrive or flounder.

EXTERNAL FORCES

These are concrete, measurable forces.

Time: When do you write (duration/frequency)?

Space: Where do you write?

Team + Opposition: Who is part of your support system, and who or what opposes your writing journey?

Skill: What writing ability, knowledge, and experience do you naturally bring to the table? How would you rate your willingness and effort to learn and grow beyond your current state?

Process: What is your writing process, from story idea to concept to full-blown manuscript?

Goals: What is your desired outcome and how are you going to achieve it? What are the smaller stepping-stone goals you need to accomplish to reach your bigger goal?

INTERNAL FORCES

These forces are abstract and emotion-based.

Vision: Why are you a writer? What does the call of writing do for you and how are you answering it? How might your writing impact others?

Real-World Self: You are a beautiful medley of characteristics, habits, values, fears, strengths, struggles, beliefs, and moods. Which aspects of your real-world self support your writer self, and which ones hold you back?

Determination: Consider this philosophy: "If you're less than one hundred percent determined, you aren't." How determined are you, and how will you make your determination work for you?

These internal and external forces all influence your work. Once you become completely aware of your personal environment, you'll discover the conditions under which you and your Muse can thrive.

For example, a writer who once found it difficult to work in the late evenings may find that, as a new mom, that particular time devoted to creativity is a blessing. Or a writer struggling with self-confidence finds their esteem improving after joining a new writing group, and now their writing is taking off.

Habits and traits that are stereotypically negative or limiting may actually aid in your productivity and creativity. Take disorganization as an example. Not everyone needs to be organized to be productive; some people thrive in chaos. If this is you, are you using it to your advantage?

As you explore your natural writing forces, you'll begin to understand who you are as a writer (Point A), who you'd like to become as a writer (Point X), and you'll be able to design a plan to get from Point A to Point X. This plan will involve big goals and all the smaller stepping-stone goals in between.

To make progress, some writers may have to change up their writing sessions. Some writers may have to join a writing group. Some writers may have to hire an editor. Unless you're clear on your natural writing forces, it's nearly impossible to know which task to focus on or what decision to make. No matter who you are or where you are in your writing journey, being "intentional" about your progress is the best way to move forward.

Just like a story has a plot, where each incident must lead to another, so must our writing journey follow a plot, where each writing task or decision leads to another.

Setting intentions based on your natural writing forces is a fantastic strategy that can help you establish the plot of your writing journey!

This means you need to have a clear understanding of the desired outcome and what you need to accomplish to achieve it.

After exploring your natural writing forces and setting intentions for a short while, you'll start to learn quite a bit about yourself. Don't be surprised to discover that what you thought was a strength was actually an avoidance tactic, or what you believed was a bad habit was actually a cool time hack.

This is another reason why journaling is so much more than a dumping ground for your thoughts and feelings. It's a record keeper for everything. You can see trends develop over time, learn how certain situations trigger you, understand how you respond to disruptions, and recognize how to spot negative patterns.

DISCOVERY WORK

The following steps and questions can help you understand who you are as a writer, who you'd like to become as a writer, and help you design a plan to accomplish your goals. Intentional writers are doing much more than simply writing words. They're writing with the fundamental understanding that the current day's productivity will lead directly toward another goal. That their writing sessions should never be treated as isolated moments in their day that have no consequence.

Step 1. Examine the natural writing forces in your life.

Step 2. Journal your intentions for your writing. Some prompts include:

a.| What is the outcome I want to achieve?

b.| In order to achieve the outcome, what tasks or steps would be beneficial?

c.| What external and internal forces will support me with my intentions?

d.| How will I apply these forces?

e.| What can potentially block me? How could I potentially meet with resistance?

f.| What is my hack for any potential blocks or resistance?

g.| What do I believe about my writing journey?

6

CREATIVITY, EVERY DAY

Many, many moons ago, I advocated for daily writing. I believed that anyone could find time to write every single day, no matter what they were up against. Needless to say, I received a lot of criticism for that stance. People would disagree through comments on my blog posts, citing reasons why daily writing was impossible for them.

I took their comments and frustrations to heart and spent a lot of time noodling over this. *Why can I write every day when other people can't?* At the time, I felt like a cross between a Jedi and a minivan, so it wasn't like I had nothing going on. I thought, "Holy cats, my life is crammed full, but I'm still able to get the writing in every day. What is the difference?"

For me, daily writing was a conscious commitment I made to my journey, and I stuck to it. I never questioned it or allowed myself a choice. Writing daily wasn't always easy, but because I felt so strongly about it, I persevered.

I overlooked a key factor. The habit of daily writing isn't forged in the action itself. It's forged in the **motivation** behind the habit. It's part of the **mindset process** that occurs before you establish the habit. At some point, I must have told myself that I have to write daily—no ifs, ands, or buts about it—and I must have had a solid reason for why I thought it was an absolute must.

Having said that, one of my personality traits is determination (although I think it veers closer to "stubbornness," she says with a laugh), and it was likely another key factor that played a role. When I put my mind to something, I get it done. It may not be pretty, but it gets done. (This is an example of understanding how to put your natural writing forces to work for you.)

Even though I believed that daily writing was vital to making forward progress, I didn't factor in that it's really an *opinion*—not a fact. Many writers make plenty of progress on their WIPs and they don't write every day.

I've since changed my soapbox-stance on daily writing. It isn't necessary to *write* every day to accomplish your writing goals. My reasoning, though, may not be what you think.

There's a lot more that goes into accomplishing our writing goals. In fact, if we presume that the sole act of writing is what we need to do to get us from Point A to our destination, then we're shooting ourselves in the foot.

We have to learn how to craft stories that matter to our ideal readers. We have to align our natural writing forces with the writing journey we've chosen. We have to study other writers' work. We have to connect with writers and help them on their journeys. We have to learn the ropes of this ever-changing industry.

There is so much to be done and while writing is a necessary part of the process, it will only carry you so far.

So, rather than stating that you should write every day, I feel you should honor your creative journey every day. This will look different from writer to writer and can suddenly change like New Hampshire weather.

Honoring your creative journey every day doesn't mean you have to be working on a specific project. Much of your progress is about creativity itself, not solely sit-butt-in-chair-and-write-dagnabbit.

Your success will largely result from keeping open lines of communication with your Muse. That relationship is built from many sources of creative expressions and tasks.

CREATIVE EXPRESSIONS

Writing includes, but is not limited to, journaling, brainstorming, sketching out characters' backgrounds, outlining plots, playing with exposition—but spread your creative wings! Try drawing, gardening, home decorating, painting, baking, or photography. You don't have to physically write to engage your Muse, and you might be surprised at how indulging in something like watercolor painting might inspire an idea for your story's setting.

CREATIVE TASKS

Creative tasks can include optimizing your schedule for the act of writing, researching, networking with other writers (preferably with varied backgrounds, experiences, and skill levels), reading a wide range of genres and authors, performing creative health check-ups, writing a blog or social media post, taking classes or writing workshops, building a website or email list, learning the turbulent world of marketing and promotion, reading and commenting on blogs or other social media posts, and working with editors or story coaches.

Of course, you need to strike a balance. While you need to interact with other writers, build critical storytelling skills, learn many (many) ropes, avoid burnout, and keep Life's plates spinning in the air, how will you schedule your writing to make forward progress and still feel confident (or at least, joyful)?

Yeah. I know. It feels overwhelming—and maybe even impossible.

It *is* overwhelming, but it's **not** impossible. You have to find that sweet spot where you accept that you're on a tumultuous journey, but you're prepared to navigate it to the best of your ability. This is a personal decision that's grounded in who you are as a writer and who you want to become as a writer.

DISCOVERY WORK

Who are you as a writer, presently? When you think (journal) this through, notice what emotions come up for you. Which emotions feel satisfying, and which ones feel like they're holding you back?

Who do you want to become as a writer? Again, when you think (journal) this through, pay attention to your emotions. Which emotions feel like they could support you, and which ones feel like they might limit you?

What kinds of creative expressions can you indulge during your journey? List all the ones that interest you, even in the slightest. Once you've got a good list going, order them from the most enticing to the least.

This is an extremely flexible, random, fluid list. You may find along the way that you aren't interested in one of the expressions anymore. No problem. Just cross it off. Add in other expressions as you see fit.

Any time you don't feel like writing, ask yourself if indulging in a particular creative expression would feel good. Then, if so, go do it! You can also include a variety of creative expressions to your regular writing regimen to spice things up.

Make a list of all the creative tasks you think you need to accomplish on your journey. You may find you'll need to accomplish smaller tasks to reach the bigger tasks.

If you're unsure of what you need to do, talk to another writer, a coach, or post your question in a writing group online.

Many people in the writing community are more than happy to give you tips and guidance.

7

Finding Your Writing Process

There is no one way to approach storytelling. Sometimes, writers dive "write" in without a clue as to what the story is about and just write, write, write, until they either run out of steam, hit a block, get bored, or feel done with Draft 0 (otherwise known as a rough draft). Other writers are more methodical, working from outlines and mind maps and discovery notes, and using that preliminary work to help them develop and reach a predetermined finish line of Draft 0.

To find the best process that works for you, refer to your natural writing forces. Explore your strengths and habits and what you already know about writing. Examining your life, what is set up to support a writing practice, and what needs to change?

Based on what you learn about yourself, you'll begin to get a sense of whether you like to work from lists, outlines, and preliminary notes (plotting), or if you prefer to wend your way through the unknown of your story, taking one idea at a time without much information leading you onward (pantsing).

PLOTTING

Writers who like to work from detailed notes, bullet-point lists, or traditional outlines are better suited toward a process where most of the story idea is developed or fleshed out before Draft 0 is written. This process is perfect for writers who need to know how things end and a general sense of how to get the protagonist from Point A to the Resolution before scenes are even attempted.

PANTSING

This process is appealing to writers who simply want to begin writing based on a glimmer of an idea and see where the story takes them. Worry about structure, character arcs, and genre conventions later! Writing "by the seat of your pants" describes this process perfectly; hence, the nickname.

PLANTSING

Then there are the processes that range between the two extremes. Plantsing is the combination of plotting and pantsing (we writers are pretty damn clever), and this combination can look like anything you want it to look like. Eighty percent plotting and 20 percent pantsing, 50/50, switching between plotting and pantsing from one idea to the next, or pantsing Draft 0 and plotting all the other drafts—you get to decide.

Whatever process you choose, take care that it aligns with how you work best.

For instance, if you're a methodical, list-based thinker, then pantsing (or any degree of it) might prove too unwieldy and messy. If you really don't know what process is a good fit for how you work, do some practice runs with each.

Set aside a few weeks (or more, if you can) to give yourself enough time and space to assess each process you attempt.

During your assessment, you should keep daily notes on how things are going. Reflect on how much writing or discovery you accomplish, as well as how you feel during the process.

For example, if 100 percent plotting makes you feel too tied down or restricted, that's a sign it may not give you enough room for spontaneous creativity. Try adjusting accordingly until you find a blend of plantsing that feels good to you.

Even though your natural writing forces are typically established and locked into your day-to-day life, many of them can be modified or changed entirely. Just be aware that trying to change an unproductive habit or personality trait is a lot of work and requires determination.

You may need to do some of that inner work before you attempt to bring writing into your life. If you're able to team up with a friend who can support you in this inner work, that can help hold you accountable.

Finally, even though you might have a particular approach you'd like to follow, you may not have much choice if your work-in-progress demands a different approach. Science fiction or fantasy stories are good examples because world-building is a critical storytelling element. Pantsers may run into numerous snags where their initial descriptive scenes about the world don't make sense when compared to later scenes. Or they didn't realize certain aspects of their world would need to be explained or established in order for their protagonist to defeat the evil sorcerer.

At some point in your process, you might ask something along the lines of, "How will I know when I'm ready to start writing *for real.*"

Well, here's how I see it. Writing *for real* encompasses all the planning, thinking, daydreaming, and index-carding you might be doing in the preliminary stages. I don't see how a book can be developed without all the stuff that happens off the page, so you should count it as part of your writing process.

So, as far as I'm concerned, you're writing for real whenever you're working on your writing.

Having said that, there are points along every writer's journey where the process shifts, deepens, becomes more difficult or riskier, or gets hazy. These turning points are as individual as the writer, and they're all connected to natural writing forces.

The best way to decide what to do when your writing journey shifts is to journal it through and/or talk to a trusted member of your support system (ideally another writer). By keeping your finger on the pulse of your writing journey, you'll have a clearer idea of what is happening and why, and this includes figuring out when the book is finished.

The "finish line" looks different for all writers and all stages of story development. A writer might decide that once they hit fifty thousand words for Draft 0, that's a finished rough draft. Another writer might decide their finish line is whatever they've written within six months, and then they come up with a new finish line for their next draft. Another writer may have to cut ten thousand words from their book in order to reach their finish line for their final draft.

Also, a writer has to jump their book through a few hoops if they want to publish for an audience. You may be happy with what you believe is the final product, but I caution you to keep a tight rein on those horses. Until you get feedback from other people in the writing and publishing field and you've been through the multiple stages of editing, your book is far from finished.

The writing process is long, with a lot of back and forth and do-overs. It's not uncommon to have a "finish line" in mind but struggle to reach it. You might hit unexpected plot holes, you might lose faith because it's taking longer than you initially thought, you might encounter writer's block, you might struggle with this, that, and the other thing.

Irrespective of whether you struggle to finish, start getting it into your head that *you are a finisher*. No matter what. This kind of self-talk is extremely helpful, especially in these prepping stages, before the work becomes too difficult and you start telling yourself that you can't.

Like with all things writing, there isn't one way to go about forging a writing process or story development. Only the way that feels good to you, that feels sustainable and empowering. That encourages you to step outside your Status-Quo World of not writing and into the Adventure World of writing.

DISCOVERY WORK

1.| Writing Habitat. Is your workspace set up in a way that supports your process? What needs to change in your workspace so that you can be productive and creative?

2.| Time/Schedule. Can you fit your writing process into your current schedule easily? What potential obstacles might you encounter?

3.| List all the natural writing forces that support you in your writing journey. How can you put them to work for you in the writing process you choose?

4.| Which natural writing forces might cause setbacks or other kinds of difficulties in the process you choose? What are some strategies you can employ that prevent these complications from getting in your way?

PART TWO

WRITE WITH YOUR MUSE

WRITE WITH YOUR MUSE

Now that you've done some of the groundwork to establish a deeper connection with your Muse, it's time to put that relationship to work!

In this section, I share lessons on story development, including how to create characters, build your world, and establish (and resolve) conflicts from beginning to end.

These craft lessons are not exhaustive. There is more—much more—that goes into a book, especially one you want to share with an audience. Not just in terms of storytelling elements, but also in terms of your overall vision. And in fact, each storytelling element we'll cover could be broken down even further, depending on the narrative and the writer in question.

Although we could spend a few hundred pages exploring the deepest details of story development, you'll be able to get cranking with a rough draft using the guidance within these pages.

Some of these lessons may feel elementary, while others may spark a new way of looking at things.

I structured this section in a way that hopefully makes it easier to dive into a story idea, though it isn't necessarily easy.

By starting with a bird's-eye view of storytelling, our entry point into the process—Point A—is rather broad but foundational. Before you can write a captivating scene, you really need to have a clear vision of big-picture elements like genre, setting, or voice.

To get from Point A to our destination (Point X), we have to weave a lot of threads together. This weaving requires time, practice, and a clear understanding of your specific story. We won't be able to tackle *all* the nuances of storytelling in this book, so I decided to focus on the big-picture elements, the bones that make up the skeleton of any story, and I break each down chapter by chapter.

However, you don't have to follow the lessons in the order that I've laid them out. Feel free to move back and forth through the chapters in any way that feels good to you.

Following each lesson, a series of discovery questions can help you develop your own story. Reword them to fit your specific needs, and don't be surprised if your Muse feeds you more questions to answer.

Storytelling guidance can only go so far as universal advice. You'll notice throughout Part Two that I often say "depending on your particular story" or some variation thereof. Every writer and every story is unique unto themselves. While all fiction stories require a main character, for example, they aren't developed in the exact same way—and this is true of all storytelling elements.

Are you ready? Well, flex your fingers because you're about to enter the Adventure World of story development.

8

GETTING TO KNOW YOUR STORY

There are three important things you need to know about your story before you can begin hammering out your structure or developing your characters and their problems.

1.| Why am I writing this book?
2.| Why would people want to read it?
3.| What is my book's greater mission in the world?

The first question is about what is driving you on this journey. Because, no lie, this will be one of the most difficult and self-revealing journeys you might ever take. If you're not clear on your purpose—what you want to see as a result of writing this book—then you won't have anything to lean on when the going gets tough.

And trust me, the going will get very *very* tough.

The answer may seem obvious: Well, duh, Kate, I want to write because I have a great story idea! And for some writers, that may be a strong enough motivator. However, I challenge you to dig deeper for a reason that holds more of an emotional connection, that is more meaningful. So, start digging: What's on the line for you with this book? What's at stake? What's the worst that could happen if you don't fulfill your expectations on your writing journey?

Your "why" motivates you to do the necessary work that helps you stay committed to not only your story, but your writing journey overall.

The second question refers to audience expectations. People read for a payoff. They want to be entertained, informed, or inspired. In some cases, they get the whole kaboodle. Those who write only for their own reasons generally end up with books that are self-indulgent and don't quite speak to a reader.

If you're only writing for yourself, then that's good to know up front, because you're in a different ballgame than writers who are creating for an audience. It's not a "wrong" ballgame, by any means. Just different.

(A heads-up for those in that writing-for-yourself ballgame: Pretty much all my guidance and tips are centered on how to write for an audience, but you can still benefit even if your primary goal is to improve your writing skills!)

That said, if you want to touch a reader in the world, then you need to consider how your book can benefit them.

The first step is to know your book's genre before you start writing. Here's why: Each genre is unique, with tropes and conventions that readers automatically expect.

Audiences who read romance, science fiction, or horror read those genres for a reason. They hold certain expectations and it's up to you to deliver.

I realize this borders on "formula" and "plot convention," but here's the deal: If you want to be published and find an audience, then you have to make some adjustments in accordance with readers' expectations. Don't go into book publishing thinking you can change readers and the way they look at books.

Of course, your book is unique and you shouldn't cave to pressure that makes you feel like you're being inauthentic, but that's why knowing **your** ideal reader is so important. Your ideal reader may not care whether your story fits certain guidelines and they may not have expectations at all, beyond reading a great book.

Only you can know how far to push the boundaries with your ideal readers, so make sure to spend time researching, asking questions, and truly exploring how to wow them.

The third question deals with how your book will make its mark on the world. This so-called "mark" might sound a little haughty or presumptuous, but in truth, it refers to the message you want to convey to your readers.

To figure out your book's greater mission, think about the message within. What is it you're saying through your characters and their problems? What would you like your readers to take away as a universal lesson or understanding? This is also known as "theme," which I explore more deeply in chapter thirteen.

All three of these questions are related to one another. Explore them one by one, and then pull them together to help you describe your story's message and why it's important to you to convey this message to a wider audience.

DISCOVERY WORK

1.| Get to know your book through journaling. What is your vision for this particular book? Why?

2.| What emotions come up for you when you think about writing this book?

3.| What emotions come up for you when you think about other people reading this book?

4.| Who is your ideal reader? Sketch them out as detailed as possible. If it's a real-life person, go ahead and ask them questions about what they want in a story experience.

5.| What is the larger, universal message you'd like to deliver with your story?

6.| Is there anything you don't yet know about your story that needs to be explored more thoroughly? If so, consider visiting the library to peek through books in your genre just to see how the authors do it. What grabs you? What turns you off?

9

WHERE TO BEGIN

Some of the most common questions brought up in my writing workshops relate to starting a story: how to do it, what things to focus on first, and the order of priorities that should be followed.

There isn't a one-size-fits-all answer because not all stories—nor all writers—are the same. Also, stories aren't built brick-by-brick, one element on top of another.

Rather, stories are created by interweaving all the necessary elements together. When you work on character, you also have to consider many other elements, such as plot, theme, narrative point-of-view, and conflict. When you work on structure, you have to tend to character, pacing, and genre, to name a few. It's impossible to decide between scene and exposition without also considering setting, tone, character goal and motivation, plot—the list goes on.

Having said that, I do think, generally speaking, it's a bit easier to tackle a story from a bird's-eye view first. In the preceding chapter, I encouraged you to explore your vision for your book: What do you want from this story and why are you writing it? This is a great starting point because it allows you to make a personal connection to your story.

Other big-picture decisions include what I call Grounding Storytelling Elements. These will help you set your foundation before you begin drafting. Depending on your process, you may want to outline story questions from that bird's-eye view, or you may prefer to write them cold, just to get your ideas on the page.

Whatever process feels good to you, make a point of establishing your finish line for Draft 0. This can be a specific word or page count, or a due date on the calendar. It could also be a list of your key story events and a general character evolution from beginning to end.

GROUNDING STORYTELLING ELEMENTS

These are storytelling components that need to be in place so the story you want to tell will work on the ground level. If you don't have these foundational components solidly locked down, your story will cave in on itself the more you work on it.

GENRE

Genre tells an audience what kind of story they're about to read. Fantasy, romance, mystery, paranormal, western, and thriller are all examples of fiction genres. Genre helps us categorize our stories under certain labels, and sometimes those labels will overlap. Paranormal mystery or fantasy romance (also known affectionately as romantasy) are a couple of examples. Genre can be further broken down into subgenres such as cozy mystery, space opera, or domestic thriller.

Genre provides a few guideposts to follow as you begin construction, and they're pretty much non-negotiable. These guideposts come in the form of expected scenes or situations and genre conventions. Readers of romance, for example, usually expect to see the lovers uniting at the end. Science fiction readers generally expect to read about innovative technology or futuristic concepts. Readers of thrillers or murder mysteries tend to expect a story with life-and-death stakes and a trail of clues and red herrings. If you don't include the proper genre conventions in your story, then your readers may be disappointed.

Your genre may feel fuzzy when you first set out, but I encourage you to not skip this step and come back to it *after* you finish your book. While it's certainly possible to tweak your story according to a genre you assign in the late stages, you may be in for a lot of work. At the very least, decide on a broad genre (thriller as opposed to political thriller or legal thriller) so that you can be sure to write a story that fits the general guidelines.

To figure out your genre, look to published books for inspiration. Analyze your setting, characters, theme, and main conflict. Make notes as needed. Highlight the features that figure prominently in your book; don't worry too much about minor characters or subplots.

For example, if your novel is set in the past (usually the significant past) and centers around a love story, then that will clue you in to the likelihood that your genre is historical romance. If your book has magic, then it's fantasy, and if it has magic but plays out in a contemporary setting, then you might have an urban fantasy on your hands. (As with all things writing, exceptions abound! Figuring out your genre isn't a black-and-white endeavor, and if this trips you up, it's a good idea to run your pages by an experienced writer, editor, or mentor to help you get this squared away.)

Once you think you've assigned the proper genre to your story, take the time to read books in that genre, published within the past three years. The face of the writing and publishing field changes rapidly, and the most recent stories will generally provide the most accurate representation of genre. As you read and research, make notes on their commonalities so that you can prepare your own story's key scenes and genre conventions accordingly.

Be careful before you follow trends. Sparkly vampires might be the rage, but by the time you finish writing your book, those popular sparkly vampires will have become talking dragons. Write the story that lights you up, not because you think it's going to help you hit the big-time.

STATUS-QUO AND ADVENTURE WORLDS

Generally, a story opens with your main character in a place they're familiar with—something that represents their day-to-day life. This isn't just "setting." This place covers all aspects of your character's state of being. Where they live. Who they live with. Where they work. Who they hang out with. Who they don't like. If they're in love. If they have kids or pets.

You want to also take into account your main character's values, habits, beliefs, worldview, strengths, weaknesses, desires, fears, and anything else that makes up their heart and soul. This detailed information relays some key points about your character based on their feelings about their day-to-day life.

I call this the Status-Quo World, sometimes also known as the Ordinary World or Normal World. It tells us what we need to know about your character at the start of the story. It's also the world where they're limited in some way.

Sidenote: As you start digging around the details of their state of being, keep in mind that most of this information is for your use behind the scenes and won't be on the page. It usually takes a couple of drafts to figure out which details should be included in the finished story.

Your character's journey will take them out of the Status-Quo World and into the Adventure World, which is where the main conflict takes place. Again, we're not necessarily talking about setting. For instance, a character might be married in their Status-Quo World but being served with divorce papers launches them into the Adventure World of being single.

It's important to note that these worlds must be the opposite of each other. What's lacking in the Status-Quo

World can be found in the Adventure World. The parts that make the Status-Quo World safe are not found in the Adventure World.

Harry Potter in *Harry Potter and the Sorcerer's Stone* found a place to belong in his Adventure World, something he lacked in his Status-Quo World.

Katniss Everdeen was safe in her Status-Quo World in *The Hunger Games* until she was forced to volunteer as tribute and whisked away to the Adventure World where she believed she'd face certain death.

I consider the Status-Quo and Adventure Worlds grounding elements because stories are about how the main character changes, and they can't change without this major upheaval in their life. All you need to get started in Draft 0 is a general sense of how your two worlds differ from each other in a way that forces your character into the greatest change of their life.

PROTAGONIST & ANTAGONIST

Protagonist: Also known as the heroine, hero, main character, or central character. This is the character whose story we're following primarily. The character we're rooting for, the one we get to know at the beginning of your story (preferably on page 1). Your job is to create a main character who wants something desperately and is willing to go through hellfire to get it. This character should earn reader interest—they need to care about your character and whether they'll be successful.

Antagonist: Also known as the villain, big bad, or opponent. You're looking to create a character (or an antagonistic force) who has the motivation and opportunity to complicate your protagonist's journey, oppose your protagonist's interests, or even outright prevent your protagonist from getting the thing they want.

The protagonist and antagonist roles are grounding elements because their relationship is a driving force in your story. The conflict generated by the push and pull of each of their journeys creates the main thread of your story. Readers want to know how your protagonist will accomplish their goal, and the main external reason the protagonist is struggling is because of the antagonist. Without that opposition, your protagonist's mission will be a piece of cake, and your conflict will fizzle out.

It's important to keep in mind that your protagonist will be one of, if not your only, point-of-view (POV) characters. This is the person who's telling us the story from their perspective. (See Viewpoints in the following section.)

For that reason, you must be sure your protagonist is interesting and compelling enough to carry the weight of a 300-page book. And if they're sharing this job with other viewpoint characters, then you need to be sure all of them are engaging the reader when it's their turn. This includes the viewpoint of any villains or otherwise immoral characters.

The characters who are holding court on your pages need to deserve the honor, and there should be solid reasons to support why they get to have a POV. Imagine how much your story would change if you were to alter the POV characters. It'd be a completely different narrative because their perspective is different. In fact, these are questions I urge you to troubleshoot earlier rather than later: "Why is my protagonist story-worthy? Why do I include Character X's POV?"

All your viewpoint characters need to draw your reader in and hold their attention. It doesn't matter if they're good or evil, they just need to be captivating every time they're commanding the stage.

NARRATIVE POV & NARRATIVE TENSE

After you decide *who* is going to tell your story, you need to figure out *how* it will be told. You have a few POV options to choose from. First-person, third-person, multiple, and omniscient. The POV that you choose is the lens through which your story is delivered to your reader.

Narrative POV refers to the manner in which the story is told to the reader and determines the position of the narrator (or storyteller), relative to the story. There are a few types of POV that you can choose from, and your choice depends on your specific intentions for your story.

First-person: The story is told directly by the main character. "I got into my car and headed to work." First-person POV is an intimate viewpoint that provides immediacy, but it's easy to overdo "I" statements. Observations are limited to what the character plausibly knows, because everything you write is a direct pull from the character's thoughts. This also means that descriptions or expositions have to be written in a way that sounds like how the character might think or speak.

Examples of books written in first-person POV are *The Hunger Games* by Suzanne Collins, *The Fault in Our Stars* by John Green, and *To Kill a Mockingbird* by Harper Lee.

Third-person limited: The story is filtered through an invisible narrator who is not the main character. "Genevieve got into her car and headed to work." Third-person limited has more flexibility in sentence structure because you can use pronouns in addition to the character's name. ("She got into her car and headed to work.") Third-person tends to be more distancing in comparison to first-person, although "close" or "deep" third-person POV is a strategy you can use to bypass the invisible narrator and pull information directly from the character's thoughts and emotions.

Third-person: Genevieve's hands felt cold.

Deep third-person: Genevieve blew warm breath on her freezing fingers.

Examples of books written in third-person limited POV are *Six of Crows* by Leigh Bardugo, *The Giver* by Lois Lowry, and *P.S. I Love You* by Cecelia Ahern.

Third-Person Omniscient: The story is told from the perspective of an all-knowing narrator. Typically, this narrator is unbiased and simply observes and then reports back to the reader (although, in some stories, the narrator may have stakes in the story world). This type of POV isn't as popular as it once was because readers, agents, and editors often prefer tighter viewpoints. Omniscient is not the same as "head-hopping," which is when the scene lens "hops" from one character's head (thoughts) into another character's head within the same scene and without just cause.

Examples of books written in third-person omniscient POV are *Dune* by Frank Herbert, *The Book Thief* by Markus Zusak, and *The Lord of the Rings series*, by J.R.R. Tolkien.

Multiple POVs: The story is delivered through the lens of more than one person—the main character plus at least one other important character. Additional viewpoints are useful in stories with multiple timelines, sprawling epics, or stories whose subplots don't feature your protagonist. However, tread carefully with multiple POVs. Use too many, and you risk giving away your whole story, leaving nothing for your reader to discover on their own. Poorly chosen POVs can also slow your pacing or deflate the story's tension.

Examples of books written in multiple POVs are *A Game of Thrones* by George R.R. Martin, *The Help* by Kathryn Stockett, and *Daisy Jones and the Six* by Taylor Jenkins Reid.

POV is considered a grounding element because it not only applies to who's telling the story, it also dictates how the story will be told. This decision will affect every choice you make—all the way down to the word-level. It's that deep and comprehensive. Your novel will read differently depending on your viewpoint characters and how they relay their stories to the reader. And to be frank, you'll save yourself oodles of time if you figure out the POV before you begin your draft; there isn't much worse in the realm of story revision than having to rewrite an entire draft word-for-word because you chose the wrong POV.

NARRATIVE TENSE

Narrative tense is the verb tense an author chooses for their narration. Even though the English language has twelve tenses, simple present and simple past tense are the most common tenses in fiction because they're easier to construct and they don't distract readers.

Point-of-view and narrative tense go hand-in-hand. So, when you're mulling over your POV choices, it's smart to ask yourself if you want to narrate in present or past tense.

First-person present tense: I run through the park.
First-person past tense: I ran through the park.
Third-person present tense: She runs through the park.
Third-person past tense: She ran through the park.

Your narrative tense, like POV, is a grounding element because it affects every single sentence you write. Choosing between past tense and present tense depends on the story you want to tell, but there are pros and cons to both. A story written in the present tense has a more immediate and intimate feel, and the readers have the sense of being right there, alongside your viewpoint characters. However, time shifts can be awkward because the present tense is limiting. Past tense allows for more freedom and flexibility, and it provides a more natural reading experience, but the immediacy of events is diminished.

Just like POV, there isn't much else worse in the realm of story revision than having to rewrite an entire draft because you chose the wrong narrative tense. Except for POV. They're both bears. Do yourself a favor and think long and hard about POV and narrative tense before you begin Draft 0.

Sidenote: You'll mix verb tenses as well as verb forms throughout your narration and dialogue, but diving into that discussion will become more of a grammar course, which is best saved for another book!

Sidenote #2: There are other forms of POV and narrative tense that you could consider, such as nonlinear timeline, second-person POV, and future tense. My suggestion is to hold off on trying your hand at anything too complicated until you have a solid grasp of the most common viewpoints and narrative forms and tenses.

Sidenote #3: Figuring out your grounding elements is just one part of an extremely elaborate and complicated process. Even though they establish the foundation of your story, they're only as strong as the rest of the story that you build. In the end, *all* elements must carry their own weight in accordance with the kind of story you want to tell.

DISCOVERY WORK

1.| If you have an idea for a story brewing, but you haven't yet begun writing, run a check through the grounding elements. Make sure you're clear on each one before you begin Draft 0.

2.| How sure are you about the genre you chose? Pretend you're talking to a clerk at a bookstore, and you need to convince them to add your book to their inventory. The clerk asks you how you'd describe your book and what other books would be considered "read alikes." How would you respond?

3.| Describe how your Status-Quo and Adventure Worlds are opposite from each other. What elements are present in the Adventure World that can't be found in the Status-Quo World and vice versa? How does the Adventure World test your protagonist in ways that the Status-Quo World doesn't?

4.| Why did you choose your protagonist to be the protagonist?

5.| Why did you choose your antagonist to be the antagonist?

6.| Experiment with different viewpoints and tenses with a page of your own writing. Pay attention to how you felt during this experiment. Did you find it easy or tricky? Were you able to capture a sense of the character and the setting (or any other element in question)? Did any viewpoint or tense feel stiff or awkward to you?

7.| If you're still unsure which narrative POV and narrative tense to use, refer to some of your favorite novels for guidance. What do you love about the POV and tense? What don't you love?

8.| After you begin Draft 0, it's worth a moment to check in with yourself about the choices you made that led you this far. I'm not an advocate of revising while you write—except in the case of ensuring your grounding elements are indeed the right ones for the story you want to tell. Run one of your scenes through experiments of viewpoint, tense, and any other element that might be in question. If you find that your POV isn't strong enough or that your genre isn't coming through clearly enough, better to fix these issues early on before you invest too much time in a 300+ page draft that won't end up working.

10

STORY STRUCTURE

There are several kinds of story structure you can use as a blueprint to frame your story. Some examples include the hero's journey, Save the Cat, and three-act. I won't dive into each one in this book, but I encourage you to do some research of your own to find the structure that best fits the kind of story you want to tell.

Some writers resist structure because they worry it creates a formulaic or predictable storyline. While there's some truth to this, the bigger danger is not following a template because you're more likely to create something chaotic, implausible, and disconnected when you don't.

Story structure is the order in which a narrative progresses. This includes the plot events, how a character encounters and reacts to them, and the change in their situation from beginning to end.

You might pose questions early on, answering them by the end, or you may prefer to present the story's final outcome in the first chapter and explain everything through flashbacks or backstory. If different timelines are involved in your story, you might decide to alternate between them to reveal clues or foreshadow events as the storyline unfolds.

You can organize your story in any way that feels right to you, but it's important to keep your ideal reader in mind. If you're writing a romance, for example, your ideal reader may expect a Happily-Ever-After (HEA) at the end. If you decide to go against genre convention simply because you want to try something new with your structure, proceed with caution. I'm not saying you'd be committing authorial crime, but some things are difficult to pull off successfully, especially for debut authors.

There are several common elements that most, if not all, story structures have.

Setup: The opening chapters set up the main character's typical day-to-day existence, also known as their Status-Quo World, often presenting what they most want in life that is difficult for them to get.

Inciting Incident: This key event caps off the Setup by launching the main character into a new situation that they can't avoid or refuse.

Rising Action: The main character becomes deeply entrenched in the new situation, otherwise known as Adventure World, because they see an opportunity to get the thing they desperately want. However, they encounter unexpected (or expected, depending on the story) complications, challenges, and tests. Conflict and stakes increase. They likely encounter a new mix of enemies and allies.

All is Lost: This traumatic experience flattens the main character because they witness how their actions and/or behavior have caused deep pain, suffering, or loss. This dark moment offers an opportunity for the character to rise up and reverse their ways, which allows them to face the antagonist for the final time.

Climax: The main conflict is resolved, and the main character gets what they want—or not. Everything the main character has learned until this point becomes critical in their final shot.

Falling Action: The transition from the high intensity of the Climax, where the characters learn the final bits about themselves and begin to adjust to their new state of being.

Resolution: All the threads laid out since the Setup are tied together for a satisfying ending, and the reader gets to see how the main character is living in their Transformed World.

One of the tricky parts about structuring a story is that there isn't always a straightforward path from beginning to end.

Rather, the path to writing and organizing a story is more or less like following a giant circle. Repeatedly. And not always in one direction. You may have to go backward to tweak a character's background or a decision they made to fit the story's current progression. You may get tangled up in the knot, trying to fill a plot hole, before you can move forward again. And then there are all the decisions you need to make along the way—none of which have obvious consequences or outcomes.

So, where do you set your sights first? Should you develop your main character and then figure out the plot events? Should you establish your story's beginning, middle, and end before figuring out character arcs? And when do you start hammering out setting, theme, exposition, or scene goals?

Every storytelling element interweaves with other storytelling elements. They don't work in isolation. You really can't work on character without also considering theme; you can't work on key plot events without thinking about structure; and you can't work on scene goals without knowing your character.

Storytelling elements work together, like different instruments in an orchestra. But it takes time, patience, and vision to figure out how they harmonize with each other from one page to the next. It's nearly impossible to get your story in tune on the first draft.

In truth, it doesn't matter where you set your sights first, as long as you're aware that eventually, they have to be everywhere all at once to get your story across the finish line. Having said that, I do think there are three pillars that make up the heart of your story: character, plot, and theme. These three elements can help you craft your central conflict as you're structuring the foundation of your story.

Let's dive in a little deeper to discover how these three elements work together from beginning to end using the basic building blocks of structure.

Sidenote: What follows is a very general overview, and you'll see that I use terminology that may be unfamiliar to you. I break down these storytelling elements in subsequent chapters and define terms where appropriate.

Sidenote #2: Classic story structure doesn't highlight many key events, but it's a simple framework to begin hashing out your story on. This is ideal for pantsers or for anyone who doesn't know a lot about their story but simply wants to lay out a spine onto the page to see what they have. If you're someone who needs a few more plot points to keep things on track, I highly suggest researching three-act structure, the hero's journey, or Save the Cat beat sheets.

SETUP

The opening chapters of a novel will typically introduce the protagonist in their everyday life (Status-Quo World). The protagonist wants something that's completely out of reach for them in their Status-Quo World—a concrete, specific thing (to get the guy, to get the job promotion, to defeat the evil overlord and save the world). But the protagonist struggles to attain this thing because they suffer a belief about themselves that limits them. (They struggle to get the guy because they believe they're unworthy of love; they struggle to get the job promotion because they're lazy and cut corners; they struggle to defeat the evil overlord because they believe they're too weak.)

INCITING INCIDENT

This is a key event that sets the story in motion. It's an external event that launches your protagonist out of their Status-Quo World and into the thick of a new situation, what I call the Adventure World.

Everything prior to this moment needs to set up the Inciting Incident in a way that allows the progression of your story to make sense. Allowing that space ahead of time means you can set up your character in his Status-Quo World and reveal important information that will help readers understand the conflict that arises when the Inciting Incident hits.

Sometimes, Inciting Incidents are connected to your protagonist's backstory. For example, if we learn that your protagonist has a bitter relationship with his father, then a logical Inciting Incident might be that the father has lost his home and the son is the only one who can take him in. On the flip side, that same proposed Inciting Incident wouldn't have a similar dramatic impact if we never heard about the protagonist's feelings toward his father beforehand.

The Inciting Incident has to change the protagonist's world completely. They cannot engage in this event and come out of it scarless or unaffected. The event has to be critical enough to force your character to leave the comfort and safety of their Status-Quo World, convincing them to take action despite the unknown that awaits them. The event is not an Inciting Incident if the story that follows would have happened without it.

Also known as the Call to Adventure, this event can sometimes be refused by the protagonist. If your story allows for your protagonist to say, "Yeah, no thanks," then you have to come up with a secondary event that forces the protagonist's hand. In *Star Wars: A New Hope*, Luke Skywalker refuses the Call to Adventure, but on returning home, he finds his aunt and uncle have been killed and everything destroyed by stormtroopers. This tragedy convinces Luke to team up with Obi Wan Kenobi.

Even if your character doesn't outright refuse, they should *resist*, on some level, this call to adventure. This resistance speaks to your character's lack (they don't believe they're worthy or equipped in some way). You want to include a sequence of scenes showing your protagonist's reluctance to move out of the comfort of their Status-Quo World (even if they're dissatisfied with it). This sequence will launch your character into the rising action and high-stakes arena of the Adventure World.

RISING ACTION

This portion of the story shows your character navigating the Adventure World. Your protagonist spends a lot of time figuring out how to work this new world in a way that feels safe to them. But it's like fitting a square peg into a round hole. They quickly learn that this world is the total opposite of what they once knew, and their past behaviors or decisions in the Status-Quo World fail to work in the Adventure World.

Of course, this means they'll doubt their abilities. They'll want to leave, but they can't. They're irrevocably involved in a meaningful way. They're either invested emotionally or personally, or they're held against their will.

As your protagonist tries to figure out how the Adventure World works, they'll build skills, gain knowledge or tools, or make new friends, which lends some hope in the early stages of their journey. However, they'll also encounter complications, challenges, tests, and crises that trigger their fears, worries, weaknesses, and lack of belief in themselves.

Depending on your story, your character might either think they're succeeding in the Adventure World or failing miserably. Whichever path your character is on during this stretch of the story, you want to hit them hard with an event that upends their attitude or awareness. This flip will pivot your story in a new direction, helping to keep conflict escalating and stakes rising.

During this section of the story, your character is generally unwilling to change their ways, and this is part of what makes it difficult to adjust to the Adventure World. The other troublesome aspect involves their conflict with the main antagonist.

You might say that the Adventure World is where an antagonist reigns supreme, but it's also possible that your antagonist is struggling here, too. Either way, the Adventure World is not designed to fit the needs and desires of both the protagonist and the antagonist. Someone has to yield.

This means that both need to continually cause problems for one another and get in each other's way. As the conflict ensues, the stakes need to become higher and higher until the boiling point is reached. Throughout this external struggle, we see how the protagonist is challenged internally. Their flawed belief is still causing problems in the Adventure World, but on a higher scale. There's much more at stake now because they have more to lose if they fail.

ALL IS LOST

Otherwise known as Dark Night of the Soul, this rock-bottom moment shows the protagonist how their inability to change their ways has led to major loss or failure. The protagonist is forced to face their situation, and it ain't pretty. They will question their choices and debate whether they have what it takes to secure their goal after all.

CLIMAX

The final major event of your story, popularly known as the Climax (I call it the Big Battle), is the moment when your protagonist has one last confrontation with the antagonist. Not only does your main character experience a final self-revelation that leads to their ultimate transformation, but they use that transformation during the Big Battle to end the conflict and hopefully be victorious.

If your story includes more than one antagonistic force standing in the way of your protagonist's goal, you need to cap each one off with a Big Battle. Depending on the kind of story you want to tell, you'll need to decide which Big Battle is only a warm-up, and which one is the real, knock-down, drag-out Big Battle—or if you should combine them into one.

The most important point of this final event is that there are no more chances for the protagonist after this. If they can't stand strong in their new self during this raging confrontation, then the antagonist will totally defeat them, and they lose for good. That means they should have tried pretty much everything else to defeat the antagonist prior to the Big Battle except for the ONE thing they needed to do, which ended up being that lesson they needed to learn.

Knowing this can help you carve out the uphill journey they're on from Point A of your story on through the Big Battle.

Another important aspect of the Big Battle is the concept of "earned outcome," whereby your character *earned* the results of the work they put in. You want to avoid deus ex machina (the hand of God entering the story) as this means your character isn't the one who saves the day.

In fact, earned outcome is something you want to think about throughout your story's development (ensuring that your character isn't rescued by an outside force unless there's a plausible reason). Your character should handle and react to the conflict in ways that show their struggle, gradual growth, and ultimate transformation so that they can defeat the antagonist themselves.

FALLING ACTION

This structural piece can feel a little confusing if we treat the Big Battle as the final moment when the protagonist has learned their lesson and is able to defeat the antagonist once and for all. What more can possibly happen?

By definition, Falling Action is the series of events that occur after the Big Battle. The action is falling toward the answering of remaining questions, the tying up of loose ends, and the paying off of all foreshadowing or clues. You can have some exciting events during the Falling Action, but those events should still drive the story toward the Resolution. For example, after Team Good defeats the evil overlord, maybe they have to race back to their ship before the planet explodes. This kind of post-Big Battle event can show how Team Good has come together as a unified force while showing the destruction of the antagonist's home base—all of which drive the story toward the Resolution.

We also get a chance to see the protagonist trying on their new self, now that the Big Battle is over. They're going to be a bit stunned, maybe uncomfortable or uncertain. They're essentially in a Transformed World because now everything is different. They're different, their relationships are different, their worldview is different. This is the time when you can show your character accepting their new state of being, and these scenes help to wind down your story.

If you're writing a series of books, you may find that you need to leave a few loose ends dangling to pull your characters into the next book's conflict. That's fine as long as your current story has a satisfying ending and your readers aren't left feeling confused.

RESOLUTION

It's easy to confuse Falling Action and Resolution because you can also tie up loose threads and answer lingering questions in your final scene, which is the Resolution. However, the distinct difference is that the Resolution is more like a "snapshot" of the way life is after everything that has happened. Readers get a chance to see the characters in their Transformed World and how they're adjusting.

This final scene can hint at what the future looks like for your characters and whether they're happy, miserable, or somewhere in between. Often, this scene is set up to show how your protagonist has come full circle.

If you're writing a sequel or a series, then this scene may be part wrap-up and part preparation for the next leg of the journey. Some of your threads may need to remain loose, and some of your questions may need to be left unanswered. As I mentioned earlier, that's fine as long as you wrap up the current story's main conflict so readers eagerly await the next story.

Above all, your ending must satisfy your reader. A story's ending is profoundly more powerful than everything that came before it—but that's also because of everything that came before it. If your ending doesn't make sense in relation to the story events, if the characters don't reach their goals without a solid reason, if the antagonist gives up, if you don't answer the most important story questions, if you don't wrap up subplots, if you don't tie off loose ends, if you rely on deus ex machina to save the day—your book won't work.

DISCOVERY WORK

SET-UP:

1.| Identify your Inciting Incident. Run the test: Could the story that follows still happen if you were to remove the Inciting Incident?
2.| Describe the Status-Quo World and why it feels limiting or dissatisfying to your protagonist.
3.| What is your protagonist's story goal and why?

RISING ACTION:

1.| Describe the Adventure World. What about it is intimidating or threatening to your protagonist?
2.| What is at stake for your protagonist? How and why do those stakes increase?
3.| How do your protagonist and antagonist meet? Why does your antagonist stand in the way of your protagonist's story goal?

ALL IS LOST:

1.| What is your protagonist's rock-bottom moment? What did they do (or fail to do) that caused this event?
2.| What is the lesson your protagonist needs to learn?

BIG BATTLE:

1.| What is the big event that takes your protagonist into undeniable action?
2.| Which characters must be involved in this event and why?
3.| How is your protagonist forced to defeat the antagonist (or solve the problem) on their own, despite having a team to support them?

FALLING ACTION:

1.| How does your protagonist feel about themselves post–Big Battle?
2.| Are there any exciting events that need to occur at this stage, and if so, do they drive the story toward a natural finish?

RESOLUTION:

1.| Describe the protagonist's Transformed World.
2.| How can you write your Resolution so that it reflects your opening scene?

11

PLOT

In the preceding chapter, we talked very generally about story structure. Where structure is the framework that gives your story shape, plot is the cause-and-effect events that take place from page 1 to The End. But even more than that, plot is the characters taking meaningful action that sets these events in motion. No matter what kind of structure you use to frame your novel, you will need to fill it with a plot involving a character who is on a "mission impossible" (my way of describing the conflict-filled journey that makes up the majority of your book).

Now, we're starting to get in the weeds, where pulling a story together becomes a little complex. You can't work on one storytelling element without tending to at least one other element because they all weave together. Plot is a great example of this because without a character who wants something desperately, but who struggles to attain that thing due to a flawed belief, you don't have a plot. Your story events will lack narrative thrust, emotion, conflict, and stakes.

Okay, so let's try to talk about plot on its most basic level. To build a plot, you need four things:

1.| Cause-and-effect. One event sets off another event that sets off another so that you unwind a chain of events that grows more complicated.

2.| A character on a mission. We want characters with agency, which really means we want characters who make things worse for themselves. We don't want things just happening to them (or at least, not a lot of that). A character must be determined and desperate so that they make poor decisions that cause things to happen.

3.| Conflict. And lots of it. Not just the obvious external conflict but internal as well. Your story is more fun and intriguing when people and things get in the way of your character's mission.

4.| Variety. Mix up the nature, degree, and conflict from one event to the next. You'll need major turning points, such as the Inciting Incident or the Big Battle, but you'll need plenty of small and mid-sized events that bridge your big ones. These smaller incidents are also known as story beats. Variety helps with pacing, plausibility, and suspense.

Let's go back to classic story structure for a moment so we can talk about how plot flows effectively from beginning to end.

SETUP

The beginning of the story is where the reader meets your main character and learns what they want and why they want it. This is your staging area. You want to plant specific information for the reader so that they can relate to your protagonist before the main conflict of the story begins. You can have some exciting things happen in the story, but without this preliminary Setup, your reader will be less invested because they won't care about what happens.

INCITING INCIDENT

This major turning point launches your protagonist into the story's main conflict. It's a concrete, external event that matters to your protagonist because they either see this as a way toward the thing they want, or they see this as a way to avoid the thing they fear. How your character responds to this event is the official beginning of your plot—the gate is open and the horse is charging down the track.

RISING ACTION

All of the events that follow from the Inciting Incident should be on a cause-and-effect chain that escalates with conflict. Your character is on a mission impossible (impossible because of all the conflict they're encountering), yet they're so desperate and determined, they do everything they can to push onward. They're making choices (usually poor ones) to help them get closer to the thing they want (or to avoid the thing they fear).

ALL IS LOST

This plot point is a concrete, singular event where the protagonist fully understands how their inability to change their ways of thinking and acting have caused a disaster. How this disaster looks will depend on your story, but it's strongest and more meaningful if it's your protagonist's fault. Without this moment, your character isn't going to have much reason to make the most difficult decision in their transformation, and it's usually a decision they've been avoiding all along.

BIG BATTLE

Your protagonist has a final face-off with the antagonist. This is your final major turning point in your plot—and the only way we got here is because your character made decisions that entangled them in a series of events that led us to this big moment.

FALLING ACTION

Plot is a series of smaller events that occur as the characters respond to and handle the Big Battle's outcome.

RESOLUTION

The last snapshot of how everything ended up. A concrete visual of your character's circumstances post-conflict. If your plot has any loose ends, this is where they're tied up so that readers are left with a feeling of satisfaction.

You'll notice in the above summary that plot was discussed hand-in-hand with the protagonist engaging in conflict. This is vital. If your protagonist isn't orchestrating or reacting to the story events, then all that action will be meaningless. And if the story events aren't complicated or challenging, then your action won't rise when it needs to rise, and it won't fall when it needs to fall. It'll be flat. Static. Boring.

Conflict refers to any opposition that hinders or blocks a character's goals. There are two types of conflict, internal and external, which I talk about in more depth in chapters nineteen and twenty, respectively.

Both types of conflict should be present in any given situation where the character wants something or is trying to avoid something, and this is because **conflict triggers change**. Conflict forces a character not only to try harder or to try a new strategy in the external story (plot), but it also forces a character to examine and question their way of thinking in the internal story (character development).

As you lay out your plot, you'll want to consider a number of factors, including genre, story structure, pacing, and what you envision for your story's outcome—will your protagonist succeed in reaching their goal and if so, how?

No matter the overall arc of your story, plot is happening from beginning to end, and it's most effective when it unfolds through action and emotion, through cause and effect. As you begin to lay out the beats of your plot, make sure your external story is entwined with your character's internal story. For every action, there is an emotional reaction which sets off the next action. For every cause, there is an effect that triggers the next cause. This ebb and flow will ensure your readers are staying engaged and turning the page to see what will happen next.

DISCOVERY WORK

1.| What obstacles get in the way of your protagonist's mission?

2.| How does your protagonist respond to each obstacle, both internally (emotion) and externally (action)?

3.| In what way does this response advance the story so your character is entrenched in a new complication?

4.| Are your story events becoming more complicated the more your protagonist pushes forward?

5.| In what way are your characters taking meaningful action? Are they pushing toward something they want or are they trying to avoid something they fear? Why do they make the choices they do?

12

Protagonist + Antagonist

The protagonist and the antagonist are the two most important characters in your story. In fact, the protagonist-antagonist relationship is the most significant relationship in your whole book. You really can't develop one without thoroughly understanding the other.

They are both on a mission. And depending on your specific story, they're either getting in each other's way or one is trying to stop the other.

Because they're in direct conflict, they each have to be worthy of the other's time, attention, and energy. This oppositional relationship is one of the main sources of external conflict in your book. They must be constantly causing problems for each other, making things harder and harder for each other until they have their final showdown during the Big Battle. Without this oppositional relationship, your story will have no fire, no narrative thrust, and everything will start to fizzle out.

Choosing your protagonist might feel easy and obvious, but I encourage you to take some time and make sure they're worthy of the role you've cast for them. Your protagonist has to carry a whole book on their shoulders, and that means they need to be interesting, memorable, and sympathetic. Someone with whom your reader can relate or identify.

First and foremost, your protagonist wants something badly, but it'll be difficult for them to get. Not only is your protagonist up against external obstacles (such as the antagonist), but they're also dealing with their flawed belief and all the weaknesses that spur from that.

Now, you might feel tempted to create a character who has no weaknesses because you think that will make it easier for readers to like them. However, a perfect main character is a boring main character—and that prevents readers from relating to them. Flaws and weaknesses are critical to making your protagonist realistic, complex, three-dimensional, and interesting.

Usually, flaws feed into other flaws, so it's realistic for a character to deal with a whole slew of weaknesses. They may be high-maintenance, picky, indecisive, and haughty. All of these can work together to complicate your character's life to the point of interfering with their story goal.

You want to make sure that a character's weaknesses are a direct impediment to things your character wants to have in their life. A woman will likely struggle to find her perfect love if she's high-maintenance, picky, indecisive, and haughty. If the flaws don't prevent your protagonist from accomplishing their story goal, then you won't be able to weave plot and character together.

When you start developing your protagonist, I encourage you to develop your antagonist as well—or, at least, keep the antagonist in mind.

Antagonists or antagonistic forces can be other characters, governments, aliens, nature, technology, society, supernatural elements—anything that makes it supremely difficult for your protagonist to reach their story goal.

Most antagonists have a motive for opposing the protagonist. It could be that they want the same thing, or the protagonist has something that the antagonist wants, or the protagonist is blocking the antagonist from the thing they want. Depending on your story, it may be that your antagonist has the initial story goal (to rob a bank, for instance) and your protagonist has to stop them from succeeding.

However, there are some stories where the antagonistic force doesn't have a "mind of its own" (nature is a great example, such as the twister in the movie *Twister*), but it wreaks havoc and if it's not tamed, controlled, or stopped, then that force has the capacity to harm, damage, or kill.

Sometimes, an antagonist or antagonistic force could already be in place as your story opens and your protagonist sets out to uproot or quash it. An example of this could be a society's mindset (such as racism) or a corrupt government, such as the Capitol in *The Hunger Games* by Suzanne Collins.

Regardless of your antagonist or antagonistic force—it must show up consistently and with increasing complications so that your protagonist is riding a struggle bus throughout the story. Your protagonist must be motivated to reach their story goal, despite whatever the antagonist or antagonistic force throws at them. Their story goal, then, must be so valuable to them that they'll do anything to get it, even if it means facing off with an evil overlord.

PROTAGONIST & ANTAGONIST ARCS

If you're someone who prefers to charge ahead with your story idea, you may not have the patience or inclination to do some discovery work on your characters. I get it. Sometimes, the call of story is too tempting to resist.

However, knowing the general arc of your protagonist and antagonist *before* you start writing will go a long way toward helping you develop your story. This discovery work isn't so deep or detailed that it will interfere with your unbridled creativity, and in fact, could actually spark it.

So, how do you figure out your character's arc? The easiest starting point is the end. That's right—if you already know how your story will end, this will give you a pretty good idea about what kind of arc your character will follow. Your character's intentions and motivations need to line up with the arc you've chosen for them, so it's a good idea to do some groundwork to help you shape an appropriate arc.

As mentioned above, it's fairly difficult to develop your protagonist without also having a clear understanding of your antagonist (and vice versa), so you should construct arcs for both of these main characters.

Now, you might be wondering why you should do this work for your antagonist, who might be an evil overlord, a corrupt billionaire, or the opposing soccer team—especially if you won't ever share this particular character's POV.

While an inhuman, purely evil villain can make us cringe and sit on the edge of our seats, they're also flat, shallow, and predictable. Big Bads are scarier when they're three-dimensional, have human qualities, have the capability of blending into the average crowd, and who can rationalize their actions.

Consider crafting an antagonist that is contradictory—someone who is socially awkward but lethal, or devoted to his children but willing to slay his wife, or manipulative but cowardly.

Try giving your villain a redeemable quality or some kind of trait that makes them relatable, as this allows them to get under a reader's skin and make it extra-difficult to all-out hate them. They may never learn their lesson, and that works great for an antagonist who fights your protagonist all the way into the Big Battle. However, knowing there could be a smidge of hope for them to change their ways keeps your story unpredictable and a page-turner.

A villain who can rationalize his evildoings also gives the reader pause—"What if the guy is right?"—and this morality question deepens reader engagement. If you can write a Big Bad who has the power to sway a reader's heart and mind, then that's a dangerous Big Bad that adds dramatic tension to your story.

THE THREE MAIN TYPES OF ARCS

POSITIVE ARC

Your character starts off feeling unfulfilled in some way. Their beliefs about themselves and their worldview will be challenged. When they learn to overcome their inner struggles, they'll be able to conquer their external obstacles (including the antagonist). At the end they'll be in a better place, personally and physically, from where they started.

Examples of stories with a positive arc are A *Christmas Carol* by Charles Dickens, the Harry Potter series by J.K. Rowling, and *It's a Wonderful Life* (a movie directed by Frank Capra and based on *The Greatest Gift* by Philip Van Doren Stern).

FLAT/NEUTRAL/STATIC ARC

Your character starts off already complete internally, but they'll be dissatisfied with something in the external world. They won't undergo any noticeable internal growth, but they'll gain inner strength to overcome or defeat the external issues facing them. The growth we see will be in the external world and the supporting characters—all as a result of your character's actions.

Examples of stories with a flat arc are *True Grit* by Charles Portis and any superhero movie (with the exception of superhero origin stories).

NEGATIVE ARC

The flip side to positive arc. However, your character will end in a place that is darker or worse than where they were in the beginning of your story.

Examples of stories with a negative arc are *Wuthering Heights* by Emily Brontë and *The Godfather* by Mario Puzo.

DISCOVERY WORK

1.| Decide whether your character is on a positive, neutral, or negative arc. It helps to describe a brief visual of what their state of being is at the end of your book so that you can construct an appropriate Point A.

2.| What is their story goal? What is it they're fighting for? The answers shape their external story.

3.| What do they need to learn or understand or accept about themselves and their worldview in order to achieve what they want?

4.| Why do they want this thing? Why are they willing to fight for it?

5.| Are they victorious at the end or are they defeated? What have they lost or sacrificed by the end?

13

THEME

Theme is a central, universal idea, message, or meaning that the author relays through their story. It's the bigger, more meaningful matter that arises as characters pursue their goals. Theme is the heart of the story—a principle or a way of life that the writer suggests to the reader. As the character moves forward in their journey, they undergo lessons that propel their character arc, which the reader can learn as well.

The protagonist's "life lesson" is universally understood. Something that all people across the world and throughout time have grappled with in one way or another. Theme connects the character's internal growth to the story's plot, which helps to make the character relatable and sympathetic as they push forward on their mission impossible.

Theme can be described in broad strokes, and this is helpful to writers who are just getting to know their story. You can start with a general idea of theme, and then after you write a draft or two, you'll have an easier time narrowing your theme to something specific that makes sense to your story.

Let's take a look at some general themes:

- Acceptance

- Faith

- Fear

- Forgiveness

- Love

- Redemption

- Responsibility

- Selflessness

- Survival

- Trust

Each of those universal lessons can be broken down even further depending on the story you're writing. "Love" might encompass family love, friendship, romantic love, or self-love. "Selflessness" could include heroism, sacrifice, or altruism. "Survival" could entail good versus evil, and "responsibility" could involve seeking justice or choosing honor over love.

It's possible that your story might cover a few different theme categories. A story about friendship might also touch on loyalty, which would trickle into the theme of "selflessness," as demonstrated by Frodo and Samwise in *The Lord of the Rings* by J.R.R. Tolkien.

As you can probably guess, the above list is not exhaustive. This is part of the reason why theme(s) can feel daunting. Some of my writing clients have professed to covering most of those general themes in just one story—how can they possibly narrow the theme to one or two?

Most stories *do* cover more than one theme, and you want your themes to ultimately intersect so they have a cohesive feel—that they all work together.

You can figure out your book's theme by looking at genre first:

- If you're writing a romance, a general theme could be "love," "trust," or "forgiveness."

- If you're writing a suspense thriller, a general theme could be "survival" or "justice."

- If you're writing a young adult (YA) fantasy, a general theme could be "selflessness," "love," "responsibility," or "acceptance."

The next step to figuring out your theme is to ask yourself what lesson your protagonist needs to learn, because that is ultimately what theme is about. (I go into this concept a bit more deeply in the following chapter.) This is their internal journey—one they don't realize they're taking because their mind and heart are on the external journey. They're so caught up with snagging the thing they want, that they don't know what's happening to them beneath the surface. Their flawed belief is disrupting their attempts to reach their story goal.

Your story is about a heroine or a hero who must transform, internally, so that they can have a better chance at attaining the thing they desperately want. Until your protagonist can overcome their flawed belief, they won't be able to accomplish their story goal. This means that theme, character, and plot must work together throughout your story.

Theme should be understated and organic to the story's events. We want theme to subtly flow alongside the external events so that it's barely noticed and doesn't hit readers over the head with a morality message. One of the easiest ways to incorporate theme is to build it into your story's foundation so it feels like a natural part of your story's world.

Ask yourself the following questions to help you figure out what lesson your character needs to learn:

1.| What is my protagonist's flawed belief?
2.| Why does my protagonist believe this about themselves? What caused it? What happened in their life to make them this way?
3.| What's one thing my protagonist needs to learn to help them overcome this belief?

Next, you want to explore how your theme will unfold throughout the story events. Using a basic story structure, determine how your character will open the story believing something about themselves and/or the world that is holding them back. Follow this through with tests that challenge their belief until they're confronted by their final chance to live differently in the end, understanding that if they don't change, they'll fail in their pursuit of their goal.

SETUP: PROTAGONIST'S STATUS-QUO BELIEF

The lesson that your protagonist needs to learn should reveal itself in the early chapters. A great way to introduce theme is through a supporting character who can relay the lesson your protagonist needs to hear—but your protagonist has to ignore or defy the message. (Remember, it's this lesson that leads them to the story goal. If they accept the message too early, then they're in a great position to attain the thing they want. Your story will be over!)

You can use aspects of the protagonist's Status-Quo World to show why they must change or be destined to live a life of unfulfillment, dissatisfaction, or unhappiness.

RISING ACTION: PROTAGONIST TREADS WATER

In the Adventure World, your protagonist should make decisions based on what they desire instead of what they need to do to change on the inside. You can use other characters or aspects in the Adventure World to teach the theme in ways that test and challenge your protagonist.

Because your protagonist isn't ready to change, they'll try to navigate the Adventure World using what worked in their Status-Quo World—and this is why they're treading water. They're not getting anywhere, internally.

ALL IS LOST: PROTAGONIST SINKS OR SWIMS

Something traumatic happens to the protagonist. The nature of this event will depend on your story, but it has to threaten to drown your protagonist. They believe they've failed, and they know it's their fault.

However, this traumatic event shines a light on their entire situation and self-revelation allows them to recognize the lesson they need to learn.

Either they learn it, which helps them swim toward the Big Battle to have a final shot at defeating the antagonist and reaching their story goal. Or they ignore it, and they sink under the weight of their inability to change, which also means they can't defeat the antagonist or reach their story goal.

BIG BATTLE: PROTAGONIST'S TRANSFORMED SELF

The Big Battle allows your protagonist to confront the antagonist as their transformed self. Now, if your character failed to learn the lesson, and sunk, this means that they lose the Big Battle and things are worse than ever for them.

Their new self is darker and lower than when we first met them in your story.

But if your character has transformed in a positive way, they have the best shot at defeating the antagonist and getting the thing they want. Basically, they now have a secret weapon that they've never had before (their transformed self), and it enables them to be victorious. They've overcome their flawed belief and figured out how to fight back the right way, turning mission impossible into mission possible.

RESOLUTION: PROTAGONIST'S TRANSFORMED WORLD

The protagonist's victory should reap some kind of reward or consequence, or maybe even a combination of both. Your final chapters will show what the world looks like post-Big Battle and what it all means for your characters. This is the lesson being lived.

DISCOVERY WORK

Answer the following questions to help you decide upon a theme that is specific to your protagonist and the journey they're following in your story.

1.| What excites me about this story?
2.| Why do I want to write this story?
3.| What are some general themes that I could explore with this story?
4.| My protagonist's flawed belief is [fill in the blank], and I'd like them to learn [fill in the blank].
5.| The message(s) that come through my story include [fill in the blank].
6.| The message or idea that I want to convey is [fill in the blank].
7.| My protagonist is the best character to demonstrate my message because [fill in the blank].
8.| The plot events I'm choosing to propel my character toward their story goal work well with the lesson my character needs to learn because [fill in the blank].

14

THE GOAL AND THE LESSON

When we talk about character development, we have to talk a lot about the thing your character wants most (story goal) and the thing they need in order to live a fulfilled life (lesson to learn).

The story goal is something concrete and specific they *want* to have (to get a job promotion, marry their true love, find the buried treasure, defeat the evil sorcerer, win the war). In fact, the story goal is a physical manifestation of an inner longing, which I tend to label "the heart's desire," and is typically abstract and somewhat general. ("I long to find true love." "I long to be rich." "I long to be successful.") Often, a character will start off with a heart's desire, and then the story goal becomes clear to them around the Inciting Incident. But this is just one of several ways the character's mission can unfold.

The character's *need* has to do with something they're lacking internally, or what we also might call a flawed belief. For example, they might lack confidence, strength, empathy, respect for others, or self-worth. At some point in their lives, they constructed a flawed belief around this lack. ("I'm too good for her." "I'll never be rich." "I'm not smart enough to do X.") They *need to learn* how to change this part about themselves to obtain a better life.

The fact this is a learning process helps to explain why a significant portion of the story is dedicated to your character overcoming this need or lack. If they figure out too quickly that they're going about things the wrong way, then the tension will evaporate in your story. Further, this internal flaw is supposed to interfere with their story goal. Only when they learn how to overcome this internal obstacle does a character have a real shot at gaining their story goal. That's why main characters learn their ultimate lessons toward the end of the book.

For example, a character who seeks a relationship but lacks confidence will face difficulties meeting the love of their life. A character whose weakness is arrogance will struggle with holding down a job, despite that being their biggest goal. The lesson to learn involves overcoming the obstacle standing in the way of their story goal. The character who lacks confidence must first learn how to believe in themselves, and then they'll be in a much better position to meet the love of their life. The character who struggles with arrogance must learn how to treat others with respect, and then they'll have an easier time staying employed.

Think about Scrooge, the main character in A *Christmas Carol* by Charles Dickens. How different would that story have been if he figured out how to change his ways right after Jacob Marley visited him? We would have missed out on all the marvelous ghosts, and the story would have ended much earlier.

You can pick from several outcomes involving the character's story goal and their lesson. Sometimes, a character gets what they want and what they need, or they might get one but not the other. In tragedies, they get neither.

Maybe your character learns how to forgive their father, but at the sacrifice of not making the football team. Or maybe you want your character to forgive their father *and* make the team. Perhaps your character is someone who still makes the team but fails to learn their lesson. Or maybe your character won't ever learn how to forgive and also fails to make the team. The outcome depends on your intentions and vision for your story.

The character's goal is what drives the story's plot (outer journey), while the character's lesson to learn drives their personal transformation (inner journey). The inner and outer journeys weave together and influence each other to create a protagonist that readers will root for because we witness their struggles and growth throughout their mission toward a goal they deeply care about.

So, a character's goal might be to find buried treasure, but they first need to learn how to become an honest person. A character's goal might be to fall in love, but they first need to learn how to be more respectful of women. A character's goal might be to save the world from aliens, but they first need to learn how to believe in their own strength.

The lesson to learn is complex because it's dealing with an internal weakness, and that process can get messy, fast. The story goal is part of the external world/outer journey and therefore more tangible. Where the character's pursuit of the goal will keep moving the action forward, their failures, struggles to learn, and slow climb toward victory will keep the reader emotionally invested.

As an example, your heroine could lack self-worth. Her goal is to have a relationship with a boy she's had a crush on for years. However, because of her lack of self-worth, she struggles to pursue this relationship. When she learns her lesson—how to love herself—she'll conquer her lack of self-worth and feel empowered to finally ask the boy out.

A critical piece of the character's flawed belief is that they're unaware of it, or they have some kind of misperception surrounding it (like blaming others instead of owning their problems). This lack of awareness complicates a character's situation at the beginning of the story and allows you to build an arc of growth.

Some internal obstacles negatively affect only the character in question (such as one who thinks they aren't courageous enough to join the army). A stronger internal obstacle is one that negatively affects the character *and someone else*—then it becomes a moral problem that further complicates your character. For instance, a selfish character who backs the family car into another car but pins the accident on his younger sister because he doesn't want to be grounded and miss his big game is an example of someone with an internal obstacle that negatively affects others.

DISCOVERY WORK

The following questions are designed to assist you in creating a character who desperately wants something but can't attain this thing until they change something about themselves.

1.| What is my character's heart's desire?
2.| My character's heart's desire becomes specific and concrete when [describe an incident where your character decides on their story goal].
3.| How and why does my character's flawed belief make their mission impossible?
4.| When my character believes they'll never achieve their story goal, they feel [describe the emotions your character might feel at the prospect of failure or coming up short].
5.| What will it take for my character to transform?
6.| How does my character's flawed belief harm someone else?
7.| How does my character's transformation enable them to finally have a shot at their story goal?

15

The Ghost And Flawed Belief

Experiences mold human beings. Doesn't matter if the experiences are good or bad, wins or losses, growth or setbacks, major or minor. They all teach us something about life, and the test isn't so much in the actual incident, but what we choose to learn from it. If we interpret a particular incident in a way that molds us for the better, then it becomes a memory that serves us well.

But what about incidents whose meaning we misinterpret and learn incorrectly?

An experience that is learned "wrong" becomes a signature moment in that person's life where they forge a flawed belief under which they operate. The experience can be a major trauma, such as betrayal by a loved one or an abusive upbringing. The signature moment can be relatively minor, such as being shunned by the popular girl at summer camp or being rejected from an elite private school. The signature moment could be a series of small but related moments that, when lumped together, influence one's misperception, such as always being picked last for P.E.

When a person forges a belief based on the event, it becomes a part of their identity. If the belief is positive, that leads them on a growth path. If the belief is negative, that leads them on a blocked path.

In fiction, we use this signature experience and subsequent belief to establish Point A of our character's arc. There are several labels for these storytelling elements, but I refer to the signature experience as the ghost (because it haunts your character throughout the story) and I call the belief a flawed belief because it is a fear-based conviction that creates major problems for your character.

In case you're wondering, yes—the most common starting point for a character arc is choosing an experience that forges the misconception that leads the character down a blocked path. However, it's also possible for a protagonist to be on a growth path early in the story, but they make a wrong decision along the way, putting them on a blocked path. Regardless, your job is to find an arc of change for your protagonist, and what this looks like depends on your intentions and vision for your story.

The ghost and the flawed belief force the protagonist to play small and safe. When you think about your protagonist's story goal, their ghost and flawed belief need to work together to hold your protagonist back from success. Yes, the ghost and the flawed belief are part of your character's lesson to learn (chapter fourteen). Until your character breaks free from this duo, they will always be stuck.

You may or may not need a traumatic backstory to accomplish this job. Keep in mind that the more intense the ghost, the more difficult the work will be for your protagonist to break free from it.

Together, the ghost and the flawed belief form a limiting and biased frame of reference for your protagonist, who will give themselves specific boundaries and rules that keep them "safe" (Status-Quo World). If they don't think they're worthy of getting a better job, then they're willing to stay in their self-controlled Status-Quo World by not filling out applications. If they blame themselves for a young child drowning, they remain in their self-controlled Status-Quo World by never being around children or deciding against having children with their partner.

This is why your character needs to be forced out of their Status-Quo World by the Inciting Incident. It's a call to adventure that your character can't ultimately refuse.

For example, a character who was abandoned by her father when she was a young girl (ghost) may tell herself that he left because she was unlovable (flawed belief). To protect herself from being abandoned again, she refuses to form any kind of attachment, choosing to be a loner instead of building relationships (Status-Quo World). This behavior might limit her from moving ahead in her career or being included in neighborhood gatherings. This psychological flaw could become a moral flaw when it hurts others through her inability to reciprocate the feelings of people who do care about her. When she's assigned to a project alongside a new guy at work, sparks fly, as well as her fear (Inciting Incident). This new, unavoidable relationship is just the thing she needs to overcome that ghost/flawed belief duo, leading her down a path fraught with conflict but also potential for change.

Often, our protagonists won't do anything to break free from their ghost until they're challenged by someone or something in their life—this could be an ally, a mentor, an antagonist, a combination of several characters, or an external situation. The challenge posed should escalate over the course of the story, to the point where the protagonist is pushed to their limits.

Your protagonist will reach a point where they'll have no choice but to try to unshackle themselves from their ghost/flawed belief because something incredibly valuable is at stake. It's also possible your character will have already lost something valuable, and that grief or guilt is enough to get them to break free to avoid losing anything else or prevent someone else from suffering what they just went through. The way this moment unfolds will depend on your story. It's a lot of work to get to this momentous occasion, which is why this self-revelation doesn't happen until approximately two-thirds of the way through the story. But, once they learn how to do that, they're free to live the life they truly want.

DISCOVERY WORK

Answer the following questions to help you find your protagonist's ghost and flawed belief, and then examine the work you did in the preceding chapter on goal and lesson. You may find overlap, contradictions, gaps, or inconsistencies. That's to be expected, and you can take this opportunity to refine your answers.

1.| My protagonist is haunted by [name the ghost].
2.| This ghost created [name a flawed belief].
3.| My protagonist designed a whole state of being based on their flawed belief, and we see this when they [describe a moment in your story].
4.| Who is the character who challenges my protagonist to overcome their ghost/flawed belief? Why do they challenge my protagonist?
5.| How does my protagonist react when they're initially challenged?
6.| That reaction escalates in the following way:
7.| An example of my character's reaction is [describe their emotional reaction].
8.| My protagonist loses (or stands to lose) this thing of value:
9.| Why does this loss motivate my protagonist to overcome their ghost/flawed belief?

16

WEAKNESSES

Sometimes, it's difficult to mark your beloved characters with negative traits. Writers tend to want to protect their characters from making poor choices or behaving in a shameful way. We hate to see them acting so childishly, foolishly, cruelly, or arrogantly. Maybe it's because we're afraid they can't ever be redeemed. Maybe it's because we see some of ourselves in our characters. Or maybe it's because we've bonded to our characters and their behavior impacts us on an emotional level.

I think the same is true from a reader's or a viewer's perspective. We cringe when our favorite characters act petulantly at a dinner party, when they lie to a loved one, when they betray their best friend, or when they do anything shameful. We berate them through the printed page or the television screen. "Why did you do that? You're so stupid!" We want to shake them silly because we know that things will only get worse as a result.

But that's the kind of audience engagement you want.

When a reader reacts with shock, dismay, disappointment, anger, or any other big emotion, consider that a win. You've successfully hooked your reader and immersed them into your story world where they care about what's happening.

You couldn't do that if your characters did nothing but good deeds all the time.

For characters to be realistic, complex, show the capacity to do better, *and* to keep readers emotionally invested in our stories, we need to put our characters through moments where they aren't at their finest.

Readers are drawn in by bad behavior. They want to know how their story people will overcome their poor choices and move forward. Will they have a moment of self-reflection and learn from their mistakes? Will they grapple for the next opportunity to do better? Or will they become more entrenched in bad behavior because they're just not quite ready to release their ghost and the flawed belief?

That's right. A character's negative characteristics and behaviors are usually hatched by the ghost and the flawed belief. A character thinks they're unworthy of love, so they push people away. A character shoplifts cosmetics her mom refuses to buy so that she can fit in at school. A character hoards money to make up for his penniless childhood.

The ghost, flawed belief, and weaknesses all work together to form an identity for your protagonist, which is how they navigate their Status-Quo World.

As you develop your character, you may find it easier to start with some negative traits and then come up with a ghost and a flawed belief to explain them. Or perhaps you know the ghost, but you're not sure how it will affect your character in a way that holds them back.

It doesn't matter which one you work with first, as long as you link them together to form a plausible state of being that psychologically blocks your character in some way.

As an example, let's explore a male character who has felt pushed aside in his family because his parents adopted a boy. This character might look at the day his parents adopted the boy as the day everything went wrong for him. This would be the signature event, the character's ghost. A possible flawed belief (depending on the story) could be "The world owes me because I've had to give up my rightful spot as the number-one child."

From there, a web of weaknesses can be spun. How would this character think, act, and behave? Some possibilities include demonstrating irresponsibility, self-centeredness, lack of empathy for others, lack of confidence, jealousy, and egoism.

For the most part, the character is unaware of their flawed belief, or they translate it in a way that justifies their attitude and actions. They blame the ghost for their misfortune, unhappiness, and general trouble—and it sets them up to behave and act in ways that hurt themselves and others.

In most stories, the protagonist's ghost occurs prior to page 1, and usually in the distant past. This time passage is critical because your character needs significant time, space, and opportunity to form an identity (flawed belief) and then operate by that code, which shows up as negative traits (weaknesses).

You want to demonstrate your character's flawed belief and weaknesses in the opening chapters so that we can understand who they are right away. This allows the reader to hope for and anticipate a change in their character arc, where they might learn a better way to live and be.

The Adventure World is laid out to challenge your protagonist's flawed belief, thereby making it extremely difficult for them to continue operating with their weaknesses.

Using the example of the man jealous of his adopted brother, he might be forced into a new state of being (which is the Adventure World), where he loses his prized job and has to move in with his brother until he can get back on his feet. He quickly sees that his brother's life and career outshine his own. The jealous man wants to blame his personal struggles on that long-ago day of adoption, but it becomes harder and harder for him to justify this flawed belief because the Adventure World will not support him the way the Status-Quo World did.

As the story progresses, this character is faced with situations that put his flawed belief to the test. His weaknesses could be pointed out by other characters in the story, and he could be put into positions where he attempts to handle things using his weaknesses, but he doesn't get the results he longs for.

If he's on a positive arc, he will eventually realize that his inability to hold down a job has nothing to do with the adopted brother and everything to do with his flawed interpretation of that singular event.

If he's on a negative arc, then he fails to change his ways and reverts back to his Status-Quo World in a worse position than ever before because he lost something extremely valuable.

He fails to change his ways . . . meaning, he fails to learn his lesson.

Theme, my dear writers.

All of this internal gobbledygook that our characters go through is about theme. The lesson to learn. Our characters need to recognize how badly they're behaving and how they're mistreating themselves or other people. They also need to see how their interpretation of the ghost is holding them back from reaching their story goal.

Weaknesses are the bullets shot from the weapon of the flawed belief, and the ghost handed them that weapon.

Until they can destroy the weapon and reframe their interpretation of the ghost, they'll continue to shoot, harming themselves and other people, keeping them stuck, and preventing them from having the things they want in life.

By the end of the story, your protagonist should be ready to embrace a better state of being and stop acting with their weaknesses. (Again, this is for characters on a positive arc.) They let go of their attachment to the flawed belief and embrace an empowered one that serves them and others for their greater good.

They also reframe the signature event. The jealous man will look at the day his parents brought his adopted brother home with gratitude, joy, and acceptance. As you can imagine, it requires a lot of inner work for a character to go from jealousy to appreciation—and this is why the endpoint of character change happens toward the final chapters of a story.

Are they perfect? No. There will be other issues, just like all human beings experience. But for the purposes of your story, the specific flawed belief will be overcome so that your protagonist can be a stronger person and have a better chance at reaching their story goal.

DISCOVERY WORK

These questions are designed to help you drum up weaknesses for your character. Remember—weaknesses are an offshoot of the flawed belief and the ghost. Weaknesses are also meant to block your character's journey toward their story goal. Therefore, you want to comb through all the answers you've provided so far and make sure they all work together to create a believable and relatable character. Keep an eye out for inconsistencies, gaps, and implausible motivations.

1.| My protagonist's weaknesses are [fill in the blank] because they use these traits in a way that harms themselves and/or others.

2.| My protagonist uses one (or more) of their weaknesses in the following way(s):

3.| My protagonist justifies their immoral behavior in this way:

4.| My protagonist stands to lose [someone or something valuable] because of their weaknesses.

5.| Why does my protagonist refuse to change their ways?

6.| [Character X] is the person who can teach my protagonist a better way to live.

7.| What aspects of the Adventure World make it extremely difficult for my protagonist to hang onto their flawed belief and continue to lean on their weaknesses?

8.| Consequences that could result if my protagonist does not change their ways:

9.| Consequences that could result if my protagonist does change their ways:

17

Motivation Drives Action

Two of the most common questions I have when giving feedback to a writer are "Why?" and "Why not?"

Characters should never act or behave without justification or motivation. However, it's one of the most frequently overlooked pieces of character development. Characters may have a plan throughout the story, but their reasons for the plan need to be plausible and rooted in motivation. They also need to have solid reasons behind every choice and decision they make.

Why does your character volunteer for the war? Why doesn't your character accept the job offer? Why does your character choose to stay in the haunted house? Why doesn't your character leave their terrible marriage? Why does your character skip school?

In real life, people don't do things without a reason. People make decisions and take subsequent action or inaction because they either *want to pursue something* or they *want to avoid something*—and there's always a reason. So, when we develop our characters, we want to make sure that they're doing things for solid reasons. "Why" helps link character to plot. "Why" helps ensure that your protagonist has agency—they're driving the story. "Why" also helps build a cause/effect sequence of events from beginning to end.

In every scene, your protagonist's actions and behaviors need to make sense in the grand scheme of who they are as a person, what they want in that moment, and how that might tie into their greater want (story goal).

Imagine this: A fight breaks out in a bar. No one knows who started it or what precipitated the fight. The bartender is out back changing a keg. The nearest bystander is a fit, healthy-looking, thirty-year-old businessman, still in his coat and tie. He edges away from the fight.

Another bystander is an elderly man. If he steps in, he's likely to be badly injured, and he just got out of the hospital after getting a hip replacement. But he can't *not* do anything. He breaks up the fight.

Now, it's easy to conclude that the businessman isn't a nice guy. But that's because we only know the motivation behind the elderly man's action.

So, what if we knew that the businessman suffered from child abuse and this fistfight triggers that ghost? He's frozen by fear, seeing himself as an eight-year-old boy who can't fight back.

Do you see him differently now?

The businessman isn't despicable for not breaking up the fight. He's afraid because he's haunted by a ghost that makes him see himself as weak (flawed belief). His avoidance of the fight aligns with this identity, and a reader who understands this will feel empathy for him.

Characters may be motivated by one thing now and another thing later—depending on where they are in their character arc, as well as where they are in their pursuit of their story goal. All characters have an opportunity to redeem or sabotage themselves throughout the story. This businessman, if he's on a positive arc, will learn that he's strong and can fight back when called upon. If he's on a negative arc, he'll end up in a worse state of being than ever before.

Regardless, that arc of change needs to be filled with believable actions that make sense. Always ask yourself, "Why does my character want something? Why do they act a certain way? Why do they refuse to do something?"

When we write characters with believable actions, our readers will care about them more easily because they understand where the character is coming from, why they do the things they do. For example, it might be tough to care about Maverick from *Top Gun* due to his rebellious and cocky nature until we learn that he's been flying in the shadows of his late father, who was rumored to have failed as a pilot. We can sympathize with him more. As BFF Goose says, "It's like you're flying against a ghost," which helps us understand why Maverick does the things he does.

Human behavior is driven by specific needs, usually things that are either lacking in one's life or that are dissatisfactory in some way. (Ah, do you see the connection to the *want* and *need* from chapter fourteen?)

Psychologist Abraham Maslow published a paper in 1943 in the *Psychological Review* called "A Theory of Human Motivation," outlining five tiers of needs. (This pyramid is commonly known as Maslow's Hierarchy of Needs.) The five tiers of needs, in order, go from physiological/survival, safety/stability, love/belonging, esteem/accomplishment, and self-actualization.

In the 1970s, Maslow modified and expanded his hierarchy to eight levels, which include cognitive, aesthetic, and transcendence needs. Along with this expanded model, Maslow refined his original theory regarding needs, so if you choose to research this further, be sure to look at the entire scope of his work.

The original five-tier hierarchy explains that people will meet their survival needs first before meeting the need for safety/stability, and they won't seek the need for love/belonging until their needs for safety and survival are met, and so on up the pyramid.

In Maslow's later work, he recognizes that many people can focus on needs "out of order" depending on their specific circumstances, such as focusing so strongly on the need for love that they forgo basic self-care such as sleep. Or, sometimes, people might try to meet multiple needs simultaneously, such as safety and love and survival.

Motivation will evolve as the character evolves, but it will always be rooted in how they see themselves, their worldview, and what's missing in their life. As you develop your characters, think about how their behaviors align with their motivations. What are they missing in life that they seek to fulfill? What need must be met in their emotional, physical, mental, or spiritual realms before they can feel truly satisfied? What are they wrong about, or what are they overlooking as they pursue a desire to fulfill a certain need?

Humans are complex beings, and our needs often overlap and interfere with each other. It's actually a rare instance when people focus on one need at a time. Life generally doesn't work in such an ordered, rigid way. (Except, maybe, if pizza is in the picture. Then, food being a sole need is legitimate.) Make sure that your character's motivations are complex and multilayered in any given situation.

You also want your character's motivations to make sense to who they are as an individual, irrespective of whether it's rational in a general sense. When your character is more concerned with a need that is "out of order," it'll work as long as this irrational behavior fits the bigger story and there are consequences. For example, if your character is more concerned with personal accomplishments than with relationships (which is "out of order" in the hierarchy), ask yourself if bypassing the need for love is healthy or detrimental to them. That dilemma alone will add a beautiful layer of conflict that can be further developed.

DISCOVERY WORK

Use the following prompts to help you find your character's motivation. Some of these questions might feel redundant to others in earlier chapters. That's purposeful. As you can probably see by now, all character details are interwoven, and you can't have one without it impacting another. That's why it's important to test your answers from as many angles as possible.

1.| Why does my protagonist want [story goal]?

2.| What is my protagonist afraid of? Why?

3.| Because they're afraid, they [describe the behavior that harms them or others].

4.| What does my protagonist need to learn in order to break free from their ghost?

5.| Why do they resist learning this lesson?

18

Character Building

Character creation can unfold in a bunch of different ways depending on your process. There's no wrong or right approach.

However, it's a good idea to dip into a variety of "buckets" when you start developing your character so that you can be sure you're creating someone who is complex, realistic, sympathetic, can hold a reader's interest, and can change in some way.

As a reminder, don't forget to spend some time developing all your characters, even your antagonist!

BUCKET OF BASIC TRAITS

This covers physical descriptions, personality quirks, habits, fears, flaws, skills, talents, opinions, worldviews, and values. This bucket also includes your protagonist's flawed belief and any weaknesses associated with it.

BUCKET OF RELATIONSHIPS + INTERACTIONS

This covers your protagonist's relationship statuses and their behaviors and interactions in any social, romantic, professional, or familial arenas. Your protagonist's relationship with the antagonist is covered here. How your character behaves with other people will largely be informed by stuff you scoop out of the Bucket of Basic Traits and the Bucket of Backstory.

BUCKET OF BACKSTORY

This bucket helps you unearth a complete history of the protagonist's childhood and adolescence, as well as any family or ancestral history that impacts them personally. While most of what you dig up will never make it onto the page, you can use this information to help you establish motivation and empathy. This bucket is where you'll find your character's ghost. The backstory bucket will give you lots of tidbits to help you decide how your character will form relationships or why they treat others the way they do.

BUCKET OF MOTIVATION

This bucket is the mother bucket of all buckets. Everything your character does and says is rooted in reason. What's the reason? If motivation is missing or if it's weak, then their actions and reactions will be difficult to believe or understand. Ask yourself what your character's story goal is and why they want it. To keep readers interested, we also want to know why they're willing to sacrifice or risk [something of value] to attain this goal.

Motivation should work alongside the information you're scooping from the other buckets. Don't assign your character with shortsightedness without asking yourself why that matters to the story. Don't make your character arrogant and selfish without knowing why your character behaves that way. Details and traits without reasons behind them will be flat and meaningless if they're not put into action. Even better, action with consequences.

The character you start to create might feel like they're all over the place in terms of goals and motivations and weaknesses. You'll have tidbits of information that reflect the flawed belief, a few that reflect the transformation, and a few that aren't quite clear as to where they sit in relation to the arc of growth.

That's totally fine.

Once you feel like you have something solid to work with where an arc can be generated, then you can begin to nail things down.

Sketch out what they're like in their Status-Quo World (Point A of their character arc). Then, sketch out what you want them to be like at the end of the story (Point X) after having learned their lesson and succeeded (or failed) in the attainment of their story goal.

Those two endpoints will allow you to create an arc of growth where we get to see your character facing the challenges of the Adventure World, learning their lesson, and going after their story goal as their newly transformed self.

For example, your female protagonist may kick off the story as pretentious and judgmental. These are her Status-Quo World weaknesses holding her back from her story goal, and they need to be banished.

The arc of growth will show how she changes from that pretentious, judgmental girl to someone who honors and respects others. Her newly transformed self then has the capability to attain her story goal.

As mentioned before, a lot of the details will never make it onto the page. But those details will inform what you *have* to put on the page to ensure plausibility and consistency. That's why a thorough deep-dive into all of those buckets is necessary.

It's worthwhile to examine your Status-Quo World character for relatability. Even though we know our character will change over the course of the story, it won't matter if the reader can't connect emotionally to them in some way. Sometimes, we're so focused on making sure a character's weaknesses or flawed belief is clear to the reader that we take it too far and write an unsympathetic character who's annoying and obnoxious.

You may be hoping that some of your character's more positive traits will override the negative ones, but character traits aren't as compelling as character behavior. You can describe your protagonist as kind and generous, but those descriptors won't matter if we see them mistreating their employees or refusing to tip the waitress.

Describing your character's traits will never impact your readers more than showing your character's actions based on those traits.

DISCOVERY WORK

As before, examine your previous answers from the discovery work you've done so far to ensure your character's traits align with their goal, lesson, ghost, flawed belief, weaknesses, and motivation.

1.| My protagonist shows their [choose a positive trait from the Bucket of Basic Traits] in chapter one when they [describe the action or behavior].

2.| Even though my protagonist suffers from [choose a negative trait from the Bucket of Basic Traits] and makes terrible choices because of it, they still take the time to [describe a behavior or habit that reveals a positive trait].

3.| My protagonist feels vulnerable when they learn [describe a moment of terrible or painful discovery] because [describe an event from the Bucket of Backstory].

4.| To cope with their pain, my protagonist [describe a good or bad habit from the Bucket of Basic Traits].

5.| A person who helps my character through tough times is [describe a character from the Bucket of Relationships + Interactions] because [describe a reason why from the Bucket of Motivation].

19

USING INNER CONFLICT TO DRIVE YOUR STORY

Inner conflict occurs when a character is pulled in two different directions emotionally, psychologically, or mentally when faced with a difficult decision or choice. Your character might be torn between staying with her new boyfriend or breaking up with him to save her relationship with her sister. A character might have to choose between protecting their family from a corrupt government or confronting those evil rulemakers over a degrading law that harms their society.

Inner conflict is most compelling when the consequences of the decision could potentially result in something negative, so the choice should be supremely difficult. To do this, focus on what's at stake with this choice. Using the last example above: If the character chooses to protect his family, how will that create further trouble? If the character chooses to confront the government, how might that put his family in danger?

Internal conflict isn't just about doing what's morally right (otherwise, the choice would be easy to make). It's also about your character's flawed belief. What is your character trying to avoid? What lesson do they need to learn? Your character's flawed belief should make their choices more difficult throughout the story.

The Setup of your novel shows your character doing everything possible to stay safe and secure in their Status-Quo World. They're living by a code fully dictated by their flawed belief. A hot-headed, self-righteous character might think: "I must take revenge on the rival gang because it's the only way to show them who's boss." If this character's attitude goes unchallenged by any other value or moral code, then it's easy for them to let this flawed belief control their life. However, because we want characters to change (for the better or the worse), another value needs to conflict with this flawed belief.

The strongest kind of internal conflict is between equally positive or equally negative values. A detective who discovers his lover is a murderer might be faced with a conflict of justice or love. A newly married actress could struggle between devoting her time to her husband or to her job. A young mage desperate to fit into magic school might be torn between hanging out with the popular kids who accept her, or with her sister, who's considered an outsider.

The trigger for this inner conflict will depend on your story. Sometimes, conflict is already raging within the character, and your story could open with them torn between two values. Other times, you might need an external trigger to get your character rethinking their attitude or way of life.

That character who's set on revenge against the rival gang might need to hear from his wife to help him see the person he's becoming. But because the greatest change is the one we make within ourselves, we don't want the wife's warning to be what changes the character. We simply want it to spark a small self-revelation—something inside the character reacts to the wife's warning, and this sets him on a course of potential change. This process of learning how to ditch the flawed belief is the inner journey a character is on throughout your story. And this inner journey always impacts the outer journey.

If the vengeful character is on a positive arc, then they undergo a moral self-revelation and finally get to a point where they learn how to overcome their bloodthirsty impulses while still maintaining power. They might say to themselves, "Maybe revenge isn't the only way to show who's boss."

If the vengeful character is on a negative arc, then they never undergo a moral self-revelation. They become worse by the end of the book, having fallen morally to a point lower than where they were at the start of the story. They might say to themselves, "I'll kill anyone who gets in my way."

There are many steps between Point A, where your character is living by the code of their flawed belief, and the Big Battle, where your character is put to the ultimate test. These steps will show how your character fails repeatedly, forced to pivot, and adjust. These failures and adjustments teach your character the error of their ways. A positive-arc character will go through a moral self-revelation, ditch their flawed belief, and start doing things the right way to solve their problem.

Because the journey part of your story will take up most of your book, you want to keep readers engaged so they're wondering what'll happen next.

"What will the character choose to do?"

"How will they get out of this?"

"Will they sacrifice A or will they sacrifice B?"

"If they sacrifice A, how will they explain it so they're forgiven?"

Your character's journey is so much more than a series of things happening to them. In fact, it's a series of things happening because your character made choices or decisions that led to the next thing happening. We want protagonists who have agency, where they're responsible for what happens in the story. The kinds of choices they make in the Setup will be different from the kinds of choices they make during the Big Battle because they're at different points along their character arc.

Having said that, your antagonist (or antagonistic force) will also be hard at work, pushing your protagonist into corners, crushing them between a rock and a hard place, forcing them into impossible choices.

There will be situations that are launched by your antagonist, thereby making it seem like your protagonist is in a passive role. In fact, your protagonist is largely in a reactionary status throughout the first half of your story. But reactionary isn't the same as passive. Your protagonist should react, based on their current beliefs, and take decisive actions to counter your antagonist. That will give them the agency they need.

Can your protagonist ever be passive? Yes, but it depends on your story and where they are along the character arc. There should be a very good reason for a protagonist not to react to something that happened. While you can have a few moments of them analyzing, assessing, thinking, strategizing, wondering, navel-gazing—those moments should be brief and ideally should lead your character into acting in response.

This means that internal conflict isn't just about what's tearing up your character on the inside. It's about how your character handles it on the outside. They're pulled in two different directions internally, and they must decide what to do. This decision leads them into acting, which then puts them into a new situation.

Internal conflict triggers a choice that leads to external action.

DISCOVERY WORK

The following questions are intended to help you deepen the discovery work you've been doing so far.

1.| What does my character need to avoid or learn?

2.| How has my character's internal conflict become more complicated from Point A to the Big Battle?

3.| In what ways has my character's internal conflict pushed them into making tough choices?

4.| How has my antagonist made things even worse?

5.| What moments of self-revelation does my character undergo?

6.| Which other characters try to teach my protagonist that they're living by a code of flawed belief?

7.| Why doesn't my character want to give up their flawed belief?

20

USING EXTERNAL CONFLICT TO DRIVE YOUR STORY

External conflict is when a character struggles with an outside force, which comes in the form of another character (such as the antagonist), a situation, nature, or even an entire society.

Where internal conflict is about a problem that your protagonist must resolve inside themselves, external conflict is a problem they must resolve in the plot.

We talked about plot in chapter eleven, but as a refresher: Plot is a cause-and-effect sequence of external events that grows more complicated throughout the story. Even though plot is about the external journey, it's largely instigated by your protagonist's internal journey. When you work on plot, you need to refer to your protagonist's ghost, flawed belief, weaknesses, and their motivations. Your protagonist makes decisions and takes action based on their inner gobbledygook. This is how internal conflict drives plot. In turn, plot (events and their consequences) impacts the protagonist internally, challenging their belief system and the way they live their lives, forcing them to undergo meaningful, soulful change.

External conflict isn't just about things going wrong for your character. **External conflict is more interesting when it reaps consequences of a choice your character made.** If your protagonist doesn't reach their goal, how will that make things worse? If your protagonist doesn't get what they want, what terrible thing will happen to them? If your protagonist takes XYZ action, how will that harm their relationship with their best friend?

Sometimes, your character might be in a position where they must do something awful, and this can feel worrisome to the writer in charge. Often, my clients will confess they hold back from writing a scene where their character could have done something truly despicable because it would have made them unlikeable. The best way around that is to make sure your audience understands where your protagonist is coming from. *Always show why your protagonist makes the choices they make, and why they do the things they do.* That way, your audience will understand the cause of the protagonist's actions without having to necessarily approve of them.

The nature and degree of external conflict depends on the kind of story you're telling. For example, a character losing his job might land a better job, but his new boss turns out to be his ex-wife. Or a character losing his job might be unable to pay off his debt to a loan shark.

If the external conflict in your story doesn't lead your characters into a new situation via consequences, then it isn't doing anything to propel your story forward. It also means that your story has low stakes.

Stakes refers to what's on the line for your protagonist. You'll need story-level stakes, where we need to know what can be gained or lost if your protagonist fails to succeed in their mission to reach their story goal. And you'll need scene-level stakes, where we need to know what can be gained or lost if your protagonist doesn't reach an immediate goal within a particular scene.

Putting your characters through difficult situations is a handy way to hook your reader, but we're only hooked for so long. You can have car chases, zinging bullets, and aliens hatching in downtown Boston to your heart's desire, but if there's nothing at stake—if nothing of value could be lost (or gained)—your difficult situation will fizzle out. Why would anyone choose to risk their life to slay a dragon if nothing could be gained or lost in the process?

Stakes can be anything from losing (or gaining) a job, loved one, opportunity, pet, battle, house, clean air, morality, family, safety, college degree, life, freedom—as long as what's at risk is highly valued by the character, then any of these (and then some) work fine.

When considering external conflict and stakes, keep in mind that there's a scale to play with. Ask yourself how much is on the line? How can this get worse? How is this conflict relevant to characters beyond the protagonist? Does this situation impact just the protagonist, or does it go higher—say, the protagonist's family or their small town? Could it go even higher than that, where a whole country or the world or the universe is at stake?

Your story's overall conflict and stakes may be on a small scale, where the trouble doesn't ripple out beyond your protagonist. That's totally fine—it all depends on the story you want to tell. Regardless, whatever's happening in your novel should absolutely, without question, personally impact your protagonist to the point where something they value is on the line. Otherwise, they'll find a way to avoid the conflict and go back to watching TikTok.

Another piece you need to consider when setting up your conflict is the reader–character bond. Let's go back to the earlier example of the protagonist who loses their job. Even if you have it set up that they now can't pay off their debt to the loan shark, that *still* won't be enough if you haven't *first* established an emotional bond between the reader and your protagonist.

This means that the degree or level of conflict isn't as important to your reader as how that conflict impacts your character and how your character gets through it. You want your reader to emotionally connect to your protagonist, so even a minor conflict should matter to your reader if it matters to your protagonist.

Readers don't always need the threat of the world exploding. Readers just need to care about your protagonist and what will happen to them. Which brings us to a two-part question you need to ask yourself: If your character doesn't succeed, so what and why should we care?

You can figure this out, as long as you've created a character your reader wants to follow for 300-ish pages. That's no easy task, and it may take a few drafts before you finally create a story-worthy character.

Speaking of 300-ish pages—you know, that's a lot of story to pull a reader through. The conflict and stakes you introduce on page 14 should not be the same on page 314. The trouble you're putting your character through should get worse (again, in relation to the kind of story you want to tell), and if you can time it so beautifully that they get worse at the worst moment possible—yup, that's a scene sure to hook your reader.

One way to escalate stakes is to ensure they're difficult for your character to accept. You want your character to realize the thing they must do is also the thing they don't want to do. If it's easy for them to slay the dragon, then where's the tension? Where's our worry and fear for your character?

As the trouble escalates, the reader's bond with your character will strengthen. We see them up against one difficult thing after another, and we see how they come out of each situation. We have a front-row seat to what's on the line for them, and the tougher you make their journey, the more we root for them.

DISCOVERY WORK

More questions to help you deepen the discovery work you're doing so far.

1.| What is the worst thing that could happen to my character if they don't take action to save something or someone they value?
2.| My character doesn't want to take action because [explain what frightens your character].
3.| How will taking action put my character at risk?
4.| How does my antagonist up their game? How do the stakes get higher as a result?
5.| How does my protagonist's inner journey drive the plot?
6.| Why does my protagonist do the things they do? Are their rationalizations becoming harder for them to believe as they progress through the story?
7.| What self-revelation does my protagonist experience?
8.| What is my protagonist wrong about at the beginning of the story? Do they learn the truth, and if so, how?
9.| How does my protagonist's ghost and flawed belief hold them back from doing the right thing(s) throughout the story?

21

SCENE BUILDING

A scene is a unit of storytelling that takes place in a single location and continuous time, in which the POV character encounters something (or someone) that pivots the situation in a new direction, changing the character's state of being as a result.

Scenes are the visual and vicarious steps in a story's plot, where we get to watch and hear the protagonist in action. Where they grab us by the lapels, insisting, "Follow me, something that matters is about to happen here." By the end of the scene, we've encountered something new in the protagonist's story that pulls us in deeper and makes us ask with wonder, fear, hope, or awe: "What will happen next?"

Let's take a female character who opens a scene hunting in the forest on a cold, misty morning. She's fulfilling her duty to feed her family, but before she can find prey, she comes face-to-face with the legendary creature that's been terrorizing the village. Our character, not knowing how to fight the monster, flees the forest, dropping her bow and arrows in her haste.

In that example, not only did the situation turn in a new direction (the character's goal to hunt was thwarted), but her state of being changed from feeling safe to feeling fear. This is all because of the pivot (confrontation with the monster).

Pivots inject energy into scenes, and they come in the form of a disruption, twist, conflict, surprise, information—anything that turns a situation in a new direction. Without a pivot, the scene is still a scene but lacks narrative thrust.

While scenes can range anywhere from quiet pulses to major upheavals, all scenes are intended to further the plot and a character's development. Scenes are constructed of two main ingredients: action and emotion.

As you develop your story, you'll reach a point where you'll need to determine which scenes belong, which ones need to be cut, which ones need to be added, and which ones need to escalate. It helps to pay attention to the sequence of events. Ask yourself which action logically comes next, and how that action deepens and challenges your protagonist. Keep track of how these events are escalating and how that in turn disturbs your character's state of being.

While you can include some scenes that are strictly "action-based," keep in mind that readers are interested in how your characters are handling the situations thrown at them. A scene might be setting up the narrative drive, but if there's nothing at stake for the character in that particular scene, it's not compelling and it's easy to skim.

Compelling scenes typically have the following elements: clear place and time, a viewpoint character who wants something specific, a trigger, a pivot, action and emotional reaction, and a change of some kind.

CLEAR PLACE & TIME

Set your scene with location and time. How specific you need to be with these two elements depends on what came before in your story and what's important for your readers to understand about what's happening in the scene right now.

A man who's been kidnapped in the previous scene could have no clue where he is when the next scene opens. He might wake up after being knocked unconscious and can only identify certain sounds or smells that help him figure out he's in a basement somewhere. That lack of knowledge might be enough to grab a reader's attention, and we might not need more than that in this particular moment.

A scene could open with a character in their office, staring out the window at the view of New York City, and we're immediately grounded in location.

A scene could begin with a character milking a cow, the brightness of the rising sun blinding them. These basic details tell us enough about where and when this moment is unfolding.

Typically, the location of your scene's beginning will roughly stay the same, but there are exceptions (such as the POV character traveling). Whenever possible, keep the time span on a continuum, although this depends on the kind of story you're writing.

VIEWPOINT CHARACTER

Every scene is relayed to the reader through the lens of a character or the narrator. If you have more than one viewpoint character in your story, it's critical to introduce that character's identity in your first paragraph, if not your very first sentence. If your story has only one POV character, then you don't have to worry about clarifying this detail from one scene to the next.

As the scene unfolds, we're getting the information from that one viewpoint character—and no other character should add in their two cents. If you drift from one character's thoughts to another within a scene, that's known as "head-hopping," and it should be avoided.

Sidenote: If you're using an omniscient narrator (who is all-knowing), then the information will expand beyond what any character knows. However, you still want to be judicious in the amount of details given to your reader to avoid overwhelm or what is known as "info dumping."

SCENE GOAL

Your viewpoint character will want something specific—generally known as the scene goal. This can be as dramatic as confronting a friend about their betrayal or as minor as getting to work on time, it doesn't matter—as long as it's related in some way to the bigger story goal. (Connecting the scene goal to the bigger story goal helps you write scenes that are essential to the plot.)

Your character takes basic action to attain the scene goal, and depending on your story, they're either successful or not—but it moves the plot forward in some way.

TRIGGER

Otherwise known as the "inciting incident" of the scene. Same idea as the story-level Inciting Incident we talked about in chapter ten, but this one is smaller and related to the specific situation unfolding for your character in the scene. The trigger can be intentional (protagonist timing her run just right so she "accidentally" bumps into the cute guy walking his dog) or it could be a chance situation (the storm knocked out the electricity). Whatever it is, this trigger sets off the action of the scene.

ACTION + EMOTIONAL REACTION

Scenes are about the basic action that your viewpoint character takes toward their scene goal. Basic action is what differentiates a scene from exposition or narrative, where we get a report or a summary of information.

The action includes a hook that draws your reader into what's about to take place. Treat this as a reader question: What is about to happen? Throughout the scene, the character makes certain choices they hope will push them closer to their goal, and those choices are based on who they are in that moment. (Where are they in their arc of character change? How tied are they to their flawed belief in this scene because that's what's guiding their decisions? Which weaknesses are they relying on to get what they want?)

Readers need to not only ask what will happen, they need to care about what will happen. Your character's emotions are critical in helping your reader understand why your character does the things they do, as well as empathize with them throughout their mission.

We want to see your characters entwined with the plot, and their reactions are a solid way to ensure things aren't happening in a vacuum. Things happen, and they should matter to your character on some level. If they're taking action but not feeling the impact from those actions, your reader will have a more difficult time connecting with them.

Scenes move with a weaving together of internal and external conflict. Your character takes external action for internal reasons. How do these decisions make things worse for them?

PIVOT

Scenes are more compelling when your character encounters something unexpected that complicates attaining the scene goal. This can come in the form of another character, new information, or an obstacle—anything that escalates the stakes, deepens the reader–character bond, poses or answers a question, or triggers or solves a mystery.

Depending on your story, your character may or may not be able to overcome the trouble in the scene. In either scenario, the scene should turn so that by the end of it, we have new information (be it positive or negative) at hand.

While there are some scenes that might unfold relatively conflict-free, treat those as "setups" for upcoming turmoil. These can be useful but shouldn't be overused as they won't do much to further the story.

Some scenes or sequences of scenes might be "detours" where the character is temporarily forced away from their story goal mission in order to accomplish something else first. Detours can escalate the tension, especially if there's a ticking clock involved. For example, before your protagonist can blow up the enemy's compound, they first have to rescue the prisoners inside, and in order to do that, they need to pull a rescue team together and get the necessary equipment. Meanwhile, the clock is ticking in the background: Can the protagonist do all of that before the enemy outwits them?

SCENE CHANGE

Because scenes are intended to move the story forward, furthering either the development of plot or character, change is critical. Look to the "trouble" that you planted. How does the obstacle, problem, complication, opportunity, or conflict that your character encounters provoke change? I talked about changing the status quo in chapter nine, and that's what we want to accomplish in every scene. What's in play already and what you still need to unleash in your story will help you decide what kind of change should take place and how it will affect your character.

The change will force your character into a dilemma where they need to make a choice. The tougher the choice, the more compelling the moment. This choice leads your character to a new goal or new situation at the end of the scene.

Looking back at our character who ran into the creature, the dilemma she faced was "Should I fight or run?" In the example I provided, she ran. But think about how the scene would be different had she stayed and fought. A character's choice at the end of any scene leads them into a new situation, so you want to make sure you're considering all possibilities when you structure your scenes. Where do you want your character to end up? What do you need your character to do next? What is at stake for your character in this moment?

All scenes should drive your story forward. All scenes should be about something that matters to your character and their story goal on some level. If you have a mundane scene where nothing dramatic happens, ask yourself if it truly belongs in your story, or see if you can inject tension, conflict, or drama.

Imagine that your character, fresh out of the shower with her hair in a towel and dressed in a bathrobe, is in her kitchen making coffee. Soon she'll be off to her soul-sucking job for the day.

This is a fairly common morning routine in real life, and writers feel like they should include such scenes in their stories because they're "realistic." However, in real life, we're forced to deal with the drudgery of everyday ordinary-ness that never adds meaning to our lives on a bigger or deeper scale. Those days are easily forgotten or brushed aside. If we could skim through boring days just like we skim through boring scenes, we would. That's clue enough that boring scenes should either be cut or revised for dramatic tension.

So, how can we amp up this very realistic, yet boring situation of a woman getting ready for work?

Conflict. An obstacle. An intrusion. A problem.

Maybe a fire truck and an ambulance zoom through her neighborhood, sirens blaring.

Maybe she noticed the food in the cat's bowl is untouched.

Maybe the water from the faucet is sludgy-black.

With those ideas, our character and her getting-ready-for-work routine is immediately upended.

She races out the front door and sees that the emergency vehicles have stopped at her elderly neighbor's home. She knows her elderly neighbor is estranged from her daughter. Your protagonist has the daughter's number. Should she let her know something terrible has happened to her mom, even though the mom made your protagonist swear to never get in touch with the daughter?

Your character shakes the bowl of dry kibble, calls out the kitty's name, and pokes around the house, searching all of her cat's favorite nesting places. Then she sees the back door is ajar and knows immediately the cat has escaped.

Your character stares at the disgusting water pouring from the faucet. The fortune-teller hadn't lied—her family had been cursed, after all. She turns off the water and grabs the fortune-teller's business card from the fridge. The lady may have been wacky, but her prediction came true. Maybe it isn't too late to find out what's really going on with her husband.

These possible scenarios are only going to be interesting if they lead your character into a new place, either emotionally, psychologically, mentally, or physically, and that will be due to the choice your character is faced with. Whatever choice your character makes should lead her deeper into the story conflict. (What are they trying to pursue? What are they trying to avoid?)

The character could call the daughter to tell her that something happened to her mom, and that will lead the story into a new direction of potential trouble. Mom may recover and be enraged at your protagonist—she broke her promise. Or your character may decide to hold off on making the call—and that decision could come with its own set of consequences that lead your character into a worse situation.

Consequences are a big part of character dilemma and subsequent choice. Consequences can be emotional, psychological, mental, or physical. A character could be wrong about the consequences they might face with a certain choice, or they could be forced to make a certain choice despite the inevitable consequences. If there are no consequences for their choice, then your scene runs the risk of fizzling out at the end—and there's no reason for the reader to turn the page.

Sidenote: Inevitably, you'll write a scene where things actually go great for your character and there's seemingly no conflict, choice, or consequence. I won't say that scenes like that are *never* strong enough but take extra care to ensure they truly do the job you intend for them. Even a flare of micro-tension is better than no tension at all, as it keeps your reader in suspense about what might happen next.

DISCOVERY WORK

Pick any scene in your work-in-progress and follow the prompts:

1.| What does the main character want in this specific scene?
2.| What obstacle/conflict/complication will interfere with the character's scene goal?
3.| What changes as a result of this obstacle?

Now, go a little deeper:

4.| Why does your character want [answer from question #1]? How does this scene goal fit into the larger story goal of your character?
5.| What emotions are triggered by [answer from question #2]?
6.| Where does [answer from question #3] leave your character at the end of your scene?

Tip: The change partway through your scene should leave your character in a tough spot emotionally, physically, and/or psychologically. They may be closer to their goal but with unexpected consequences. Or, they may be further from their goal, and they have to adjust their plan. The unexpected consequences or the adjustment will lead to your character's next scene goal.

22

SETTING

Your story setting establishes the time and place where the plot events of your story occur. Setting is the "when" and "where" your characters live and engage with the story events.

Many aspects comprise the setting. Not only does it serve as an expression of your characters and the way they live their lives, but it also grounds your plot, creates mood, and hints at your story's theme.

Setting and world-building are similar in that they both do the abovementioned jobs. However, world-building goes much deeper and broader because you're fictionalizing an entire universe. Fantasy, science fiction, and dystopian novels are examples of stories where the author usually creates a world from scratch that will include (but is not limited to) imagined cultures, geography, species, histories, laws, magic or technology systems, and political dynamics.

Regardless, your story world (no matter how fictionalized) should express your protagonist's inner turmoil including their ghost, flawed belief, story goal, and weaknesses. The story world can help you define your main character as well as the entire cast.

SETTING + THEME

Theme is the universal message underscoring your story. Generally speaking, authors should avoid hitting their readers over the head with that message. Therefore, storytelling elements, such as setting, are a great vehicle to deliver theme.

In *To Kill a Mockingbird*, the fictional setting of 1930s Maycomb, Alabama emphasizes the central messages of racism, injustice, childhood innocence, and fighting for those who can't. We see these themes play out through the perspectives of siblings Scout and Jem when they witness their father defend unjustly accused Tom Robinson.

SETTING + CHARACTERS

Setting is the physical expression of your characters. This means that your story world can reflect and influence your characters' goals, motivations, beliefs, and choices. When we consider that characters begin the story in their Status-Quo World already feeling dissatisfied with something in their state of being, then we can use setting to shape our characters' arcs toward growth, stagnation, or decline.

What is your character lacking in their Status-Quo World? Is it a relationship? Acceptance? Meaning? Safety? Whatever it is, they should be seeking it in their Adventure

World. You can use this transition to help your character break free from not just the physical limitations of the world they know, but the psychological and emotional limitations as well.

Going back to the example of To Kill a Mockingbird, Scout's loss of innocence is dramatically and painfully reflected through her experience of racism and injustice. The setting of a small town in a part of the country known for its immoral treatment of Black people helps to create a realistic and authentic stage for Scout's character arc. Her faith in humanity is tested, and by the end, her faith in humanity perseveres despite the tragic outcome of story events.

By contrast, Scout's brother Jem becomes jaded by his experience with the same events and ends the story disillusioned with humanity.

SETTING + PLOT

Setting should be a logical arena for your story events. The plot that unfolds from one scene to the next should make sense in relation to the time and place where these events are happening.

Your setting may change frequently depending on your particular story. Each time it does, double-check all aspects of the setting, including (but not limited to) culture, weather, political dynamics, time passage, props, geographical details, and characters.

Setting and plot can work together to drive your characters forward, hinder them, or reroute them in their

Adventure World. Pacing and stakes are also affected by how the setting and plot are used. For example, a thriller writer can use a power outage in the dead of winter to create a sequence of high-stakes scenes where the main character is being hunted by a serial killer.

SETTING + MOOD

Setting creates mood through various factors such as weather, character emotions, and physical or geographical details. For example, in Stephen King's *Misery*, dread is evoked through the erratic and obsessive character of Annie. The feeling of dread increases when we understand that Paul, Annie's hobbled and bed-bound "guest," is utterly and completely at her mercy in her home's remote location.

As discussed in chapter twenty-five, mood can change depending on what's happening in any given scene. Often, mood is dependent on your viewpoint character's expectations or ingrained beliefs about a particular subject. So, when you're setting up a location or a time period to evoke a certain mood or atmosphere, it's important to consider the viewpoint character's perspective and make sure it all aligns.

SETTING + THE READER

Setting can influence reader emotions and expectations, but remember that a reader's expectations start with the story's genre. So, your setting will be defined largely by your chosen genre.

A reader who picks up a historical romance set during WWII will expect to read about people involved in the war in some way. Maybe the male protagonist is a soldier sent off to fight in France, where he meets the love interest. Another possible storyline that would fit reader expectations could follow a couple who is torn apart by the war.

Because the time period is WWII, the reader might expect to see war-torn Europe or what life was like in Midwest America—a region untouched physically by the war, but whose people were scarred psychologically and emotionally.

In addition to physical and geographical details, readers will anticipate scenes that show 1940s culture, lifestyles, and political dynamics. They may expect graphic battle scenes, or scenes that show details of a battle's aftermath, including bodily injury, human suffering, and death. And because the genre is romance, the theme of love will be highly anticipated. A writer might use a variety of locations to set the stage for this romance—a hospital where a wounded soldier falls in love with his nurse, or a bombed neighborhood where unread love letters are destroyed.

BREAKDOWN OF SETTING

All settings have meaning attached to them, so your choices need to be deliberate. Keep in mind that setting is typically described through the POV character, and they're going to have certain judgments or beliefs attached to their surroundings (see chapter on tone and mood), which can reflect back onto that character. Pay careful attention to your word choice. Setting can work to reveal more about your character than what your character is able to do on their own.

Setting is a web of many elements. It's nearly impossible to map out a country, town, or even a two-bedroom apartment without considering dynamics like atmosphere, character emotions, story events, or conflict. All the different facets of setting, when woven together, create a certain kind of story that will need to be authentic down to every word choice.

Consider how your chosen setting (down to its finest details) expresses your characters, the plot, a reader's expectations, mood, or theme. In this day and age of Google, some writers find it helpful to search for images online of places that fit what they're going after and use those visual references when writing descriptions and creating the setting.

PLACE/LOCATION

Where does your story begin? Does it evolve in the same place? What other places do you include? Where does it end?

Place will include anything from the planet your characters are conquering, to the city they're protecting, to the fields they're torching, to the church they're seeking refuge in, to the ballpark they're winning games in, to the sea where they're stranded, to the kitchen where they're practicing for a baking contest, to the phone booth where they're waiting for an important call (or changing into a superhero outfit).

The location of your story will generally have one overall "grand arena," and that arena will have sub-worlds. For example, in *Finding Nemo*, the grand arena is Australia's Great Barrier Reef. We see how this arena has safe and dangerous aspects based on its many varied sub-worlds.

One such sub-world is an anemone, which is Nemo's home. The anemone is in a coral reef, which could be described as Nemo's "neighborhood," and this is where he's expected to live his entire life because it's safe.

The boundaries of Nemo's Status-Quo World are made explicitly clear by the "drop-off," which is considered dangerous by the characters who live in the reef.

We see more of the arena when Nemo is accidentally captured by a fishing net, and all of the subsequent settings are related to the story events. Not only do we travel through the vast and dangerous ocean, but we're also transported to the sub-worlds of Sydney Harbor and even a dentist's office—all of which make marvelous sense because of the way the plot unfolds.

As the story progresses, we explore settings that include the submarine, the shark chase, the blue whale, the fish tank, and the sewage plant. Each setting in this film exists for a specific reason, whether it's advancing the plot, raising the stakes, challenging the character, establishing the mood, meeting reader expectations, or emphasizing the theme.

Can there be too many or too few settings? Yes. Yes, indeed. Not something to worry about in your rough draft, but it's a good idea to make a list of all the places where your story happens and ask yourself if your setting satisfies any of the above criteria. Whenever you're able to use one place for multiple jobs, do it. You get so much more depth and richness from your story when you can show a place's value and function from varying perspectives or for different reasons.

Place and location can be defined further as natural or human-made.

Natural Places

Natural settings have to do with the environment such as forests, mountains, bodies of water, outer space, deserts, jungles, and any characteristics associated with each. In *Finding Nemo*, a wide variety of fish and plant life were necessary details used to support the grand arena of the Great Barrier Reef.

When you start crafting a natural setting, don't forget to consider weather, including seasons, and how it can help to set mood, advance the plot, or express character relationships.

Human-Made Places

All human-made constructs such as buildings, bridges, roads, cities, and boundaries can be used to express culture, human relationships, and society.

In *Finding Nemo*, a dentist's office was one of the human-made settings—specifically, a fish tank in the office. This setting helped express the conflict between humans and nature, as well as the overarching theme of trust and family.

TIME

Not only should you know the time period of your story, but you might also need to know the days of the week that certain events occur, the span of months that passes, or what hour of the day two characters battle it out in front of a saloon.

Time grounds your reader because this is how we're able to track your story from one scene to the next, or even in comparison to real-life events (depending on your genre). Many fictional stories use time to help define cultural events, political systems, agriculture, and advances in technology, which readers can use to draw parallels and ask themselves story questions.

CULTURE

Culture is represented in the setting because it covers a wide range of daily living practices and social norms or rules that dictate your characters' lifestyles and behaviors. Customs, traditions, laws (including magic systems), national holidays, education, technology, social systems, history, family systems, transportation, political systems, agriculture, prejudices or biases, and financial systems are all categories that fall under "culture."

SETTING CHARACTERISTICS

All settings should be fleshed out with visceral detail. Consider all the senses when you're developing any setting in your story. This includes background characters, props, and anything that triggers the senses.

Background Characters
These are the unnamed, barely described characters that work your setting for you. The cashiers in the market, the policeman holding back the crowd, the crowd being restrained by the policeman, the students milling in the hallway between classes.

Props
These are the physical objects that bring your scene to life, making it three-dimensional and authentic. The barware in a bar; furniture in a living room; diapers and rattles in a nursery.

Sensory Images
This refers to anything that appeals to the senses of sight, sound, smell, taste, and touch. Characters should be interacting with their surroundings: picking up broken pieces of a plate, caressing a weapon, petting a stray dog, biting into a mouth-watering pepperoni pizza, flirting with the bartender. These kinds of interactions should be described with sounds, smells, or any other sensory image.

While there is an infinite number of characteristics in any given setting, only include the ones that matter to the scene in question. Details that ground your reader in the authenticity of your story as well as help express the storyline, characters, mood, or theme.

DISCOVERY WORK

For your own author notes that you can refer to as you construct your story, design a "map" of your arena, its sub-worlds, and all the possibilities and details within. Don't forget to include things like weather, props, other characters/species, architecture, and uses of time.

This map can be written out in bullet-point lists, illustrated, or structured in any way that works for you. The objective is to dream a wide arena, but then drill it down to what is absolutely necessary for your story. You might know certain details of your setting that don't need to ever be put on the page, but it's helpful to have notes at hand while you're working on the story.

23

SHOWING VERSUS TELLING

Notice the title of this chapter isn't "Show, Don't Tell," which is advice that I grew up hearing. However, that advice is misleading. "Telling" gets a bad rap because it's often used incorrectly or when we should be "showing" instead. However, "telling" can be useful. You want to ask yourself whether the passage in question is a candidate for "showing" or "telling" based on the jobs the passage needs to accomplish. There's a balance to be struck, and that balance depends on your particular story and all that's in play.

First, let's define each of these storytelling elements.

TELLING

Telling summarizes what is happening through reporting or reflection of either the viewpoint character or the narrator (exposition or narration). Broad strokes of information externalize the events for the reader, so it can cover a lot of ground in just a few snappy sentences. Or telling can be drawn out with intricate detailed information that could last for multiple passages.

Telling is a good choice when you want to cut to the chase or deliver a lot of information in one fell swoop.

Anytime minor information needs to be relayed so that the plot feels plausible but won't clash with more important information, tell it instead of showing it. If you need to move your characters quickly from one point to the next but still relay information to the reader, tell it.

Finally, some characters' or narrators' voices are more suited to the direct, no-nonsense, spare-me-the-details vibe of telling—don't shy away from telling at the expense of voice.

An inherent danger with telling is that it's passive and distant and tends to go into unnecessary detail.

At its foundation, there's nothing wrong with telling; however, it must be used strategically and with a light touch because it can generate a distant, emotionless reading experience.

WHEN TELLING IS FAVORABLE

1.| Look for places where you're relaying factual information. These are moments where you can cut to the chase and simply state the facts. This also includes passages where your character is making an observation that is factual. (If the observation is based in opinion, that might be better off "shown" because emotion—and maybe even the flawed belief—are tied to opinions.)

2.| Backstory, background, or history. If these passages are included because they're relevant to the scene but not the focus of it, then they may be best told, especially if the reader's senses don't need to be engaged or the reader doesn't need to be immersed in this information.

3.| Redundant pieces of information, emotion, or details. Either cut them entirely or rework them to simple telling statements if you feel the reader needs a quick reminder of the situation.

SHOWING

Showing activates a scene or passage of exposition through emotion, description, and context. This tool is used to strengthen relationship interactions, express emotion, construct your world, highlight the "why," tone, mood, and even genre. Showing is also used to immerse the reader in what is unfolding on the page. They feel like they're part of the story, that they're in the story world and interacting with your story people.

When we're dealing with emotion on the page, we need to avoid saying what the character is feeling and instead dive straight into the core that holds all the meaning of the moment.

Showing can work against you if you're aiming for a faster pace or if the detail is unnecessary or redundant.

WHEN SHOWING IS FAVORABLE

1.| Any time you have emotion, show it. This helps keep your reader immersed in your world and invested in your characters.
2.| Character relationships. We want to see and hear and feel characters interacting with each other. This overlaps with emotion, as most people can't interact with each other without expressing some kind of emotion. However, there are those moments when emotion might be absent between people. You can show a lack of emotion through body language, facial expressions, and other imagery.
3.| Descriptions that make up your world and how the world works to benefit or hinder your characters. World-building isn't just for fantasy or science fiction—even if your setting is downtown Boston or a public elementary school, readers want to be there as deeply as possible. Sensory details are a great way to show your world to readers.

WEAVING SHOWING AND TELLING TOGETHER

Scenes and passages of exposition aren't "all showing" or "all telling." Really, they're made up of a combination of both—but the tricky part is figuring out that balance for maximum reader engagement.

Let's try it out:

Marcus bent over the rough worktable. Wood shavings scented the otherwise stale, humid air in his shop.

These opening lines ground the reader in the scene through character, setting, and sensory details of smell and texture. Setting up the scene with clear information helps to invite the reader into the moment; however, there isn't much here that particularly connects us to the character.

He squinted at the misshapen hunk of wood on his table and sighed heavily. All around him, wood carvings mocked him. Another weekend come and gone without a sale.

Now we have some character emotion. Body language combined with reflection. We understand the character's situation. The word "mocked" is a clue to his emotional state, and the following sentence reveals why.

Outside his shop, voices yelled. Marcus tensed. Already? It's not even noon. He walked across the floor, kicking up shavings with each heavy-footed step. Marcus glanced out his open window toward the neighbor's house. Marcus saw them up on the deck. She was in her ratty dressing gown, hair still uncombed. He was shirtless, skin lobster-red from working on the docks.

Here, we've introduced additional conflict. The character's situation has been disrupted by an unwelcome fight. We know through Marcus's thoughts that the neighbors' fighting is typical, but not at this time of day. Through Marcus's observations of the characters, we learn that he's familiar with their habits and general lifestyle.

Marcus wondered where Sammy was. He frowned as he searched the toy-littered yard. There, in the plastic sandbox.

Sammy's bony shoulders were hunched, his head bowed low, his shovel digging into the sand in a slow rhythm. Marcus's throat tightened as a flash of himself at that age shot through his mind. He opened the door to his shop and whistled their tune. Sammy's head popped up and he grinned. Marcus waved him over, and Sammy dashed across the yard, barefoot and looking like he hadn't eaten in days. Probably hadn't. The couple continued to yell back and forth, neither of them noticing their kid taking off. Marcus's heart clenched.

Here, we see that Marcus has offered refuge to Sammy before, who responds with relief, happiness, and gratefulness. We also get a brief piece of backstory: Marcus sympathizes with Sammy not just because of the boy's circumstances, but also because Marcus experienced something similar in his own childhood. Marcus has some thoughts about the situation, clearly disgusted by the treatment of Sammy. We can draw some conclusions about Marcus as a character based on this one scene.

Let's put it all together. Showing will be in normal text, and telling will be in bold text:

Marcus bent over the rough worktable. Wood shavings scented the otherwise stale, humid air in his shop. He squinted at the misshapen hunk of wood on his table and sighed heavily. All around him, wood carvings mocked him. **Another weekend come and gone without a sale.**

Outside his shop, voices yelled. Marcus tensed. Already? It's not even noon. He walked across the floor, kicking up shavings with each heavy-footed step. Marcus glanced out his open window toward the neighbor's dingy trailer. **Marcus saw them up on the stoop.** She was in her ratty dressing gown, hair still uncombed. He was shirtless, skin lobster-red from working on the docks.

Marcus wondered where Sammy was. He frowned as he searched the toy-littered yard. There, in the plastic sandbox. Sammy's bony shoulders were hunched, his head bowed low, his shovel digging into the sand in a slow rhythm. Marcus's throat tightened as a flash of himself at that age shot through his mind. He opened the door to his shop and whistled their tune. Sammy's head popped up and he grinned.

Marcus waved him over, and Sammy dashed across the yard, barefoot and looking like he hadn't eaten in days. Probably hadn't. **The couple continued to yell back and forth, neither of them noticing their kid taking off.** Marcus's heart clenched.

Most of this scene is shown, not told. There are, admittedly, a couple of sentences that are half-shown and half-told, but even those relay a sensory detail or image. However, a few telling statements kept us informed about things we needed to know to understand character emotion or the physical setting, and to keep the scene actively moving forward.

It could be argued that some of Marcus's internals are more telling than showing. For example, *Already? It's not even noon.* While he's stating a fact (time of day), his thought is drenched in emotion. The time of day is meaningful due to the context of the event—the couple having a fight outside on their stoop.

Overall, the scene is shown through sensory details, imagery, character emotion, character interaction, and thoughts. This is what immerses us in the scene and helps us to understand who Marcus is as a character. The bits of telling help provide context to Marcus's emotions and the actions that he takes.

Showing versus telling demands a balance. Your scenes and passages of exposition should be a combination of both for maximum reader engagement. You want your story to flow in a way that gives your reader the right amount of information they need to stay immersed in your world but also keeps them progressing through your story to the next scene. Too much showing will slow your pacing because of heavy detail and imagery, whereas too much telling will distance and disengage your reader.

DISCOVERY WORK

Note: This exercise is best used for scenes or passages that you have already shaped and revised—in other words, you may not get much value out of this exercise if you try to apply it to something in your rough draft. However, this exercise can help you foresee what you'll need to consider or pay attention to in terms of showing and telling.

Turn to a particular passage or scene in your WIP. Ask yourself: What do I want the reader to take away from this passage? Emotion or Information? Maybe a little of both?

- Highlight in yellow any words/sentences that deal with emotion.

- Highlight in blue any words/sentences that deal with information.

- Highlight in a different color any sentences that are a combination of both.

Anything marked in yellow should be "shown" to your reader, while anything marked in blue should be "told" to your reader. Those that are a combo are pretty much up for grabs depending on the balance you're already striking with showing and telling.

To start, aim for a 70/30 split (70 percent showing and 30 percent telling), and then read it out loud to get a sense of voice, pacing, world-building, and character. What's coming through strongly? What needs more amplifying? What is getting buried? Is there too much focus on minor or inconsequential details?

Ask yourself the main objective of this scene or passage and decide if the split needs to be modified. Maybe an 80/20 or 90/10 balance will serve the scene better, especially if it's a major turning point in your story. Or maybe it's a passage that really needs to move along at a speedier clip, in which case try for a 30/70 split.

24

ART OF SUSPENSE

When we think of suspense, it's easy to imagine psychological thrillers, horror, action-adventure, and war stories.

But suspense can be found in all genres, in any story, and it isn't just about life-and-death stakes.

Suspense is where the reader is left toeing a tight line of tension because we just don't know what's about to happen to the character physically, emotionally, psychologically, or mentally.

- A character with a phobia of creepy, crawly things must rescue a young boy who has fallen into a pit of scorpions.

- A soccer player must score to win the game and help her team move on to the playoffs.

- There's a serial killer on the loose in the city, and a blizzard knocks out the power in the middle of the night.

- A young musician performs a solo at Carnegie Hall and experiences stage fright.

- The boy with a speech impediment has been practicing in front of the mirror to ask a certain girl out on a date, and finally gets his chance.

In these examples above, you can see that suspense can be created through a combination of character performance, character weakness, external situations, ticking clocks, and character desires.

That edge-of-your-seat feeling is all about knowing that something bad is potentially on its way. We don't know when or how or if it will strike, but we know something valuable is at risk. We read onward with a combination of hope and dread.

But even the most expertly written suspense-filled scenes won't hook a reader if they don't first care about the character(s) involved. This is partly accomplished through knowing the character's weakness (what is holding them back), understanding their story goal (or the goal of the moment), their reasons for wanting the goal, and what's at stake if they fail.

In the soccer player example above, a reader is more likely to be worried about the character's performance if we already know that she's an elite player, but she's been struggling all season. Playoffs are at stake. If she fails, they don't make the playoffs. Same with the boy who's anxious over his speech impediment. We're more likely to be anxious right alongside him if we see him practicing in the mirror a few times prior to his big chance. His seventh-grade crush is on the line. If he fails, he loses his chance to go out with the girl.

Authors can use this emotional connection to get a reader's hopes up when things go well for the character, and then to cruelly dash those hopes to the unforgiving earth when things don't go well. When our beloved characters are experiencing a situation that brings them misery, embarrassment, distress, grief, anxiety, or any kind of trouble that puts a target on their backs, that raises the suspense factor—we wonder how badly this can go, and we keep turning the pages with anxiety, fear, dread, or worry.

Once an emotional connection is established, then it's a matter of escalating the degrees of danger for your character. (Again, when I use words like "danger," remember that I'm not solely talking life and death. The boy asking the girl out feels a sense of danger in that he could stutter and mumble, and she could end up laughing at him. For the boy, that's a dangerous scenario.)

How you go about escalating the degrees of danger is a matter of pacing. You'll need to make decisions about where to plant clues or foreshadow imminent trouble, how to raise the stakes, when to introduce more (mostly terrible) possibilities, how to draw out the tension, and when to wallop your reader with the moment they've been dreading.

Pacing is a storytelling element that impacts the book from one chapter to the next, but also from the beginning to the end of a scene. A thriller tends to have a rapid, can't-catch-your-breath pace, whereas a historical romance's pace will be more languorous. However, even in these extremes, a thriller will need to have some slower scenes so that the reader has an opportunity to digest what's happening, and a romance will need to quicken the pace in some scenes to keep the reader on their toes.

Suspenseful scenes are the ones where anticipation and expectation are built to a crescendo. But once you start dropping clues and breadcrumbs and foreshadow terrible things, it's easy to fall into the trap of predictability. Readers immediately know that the serial killer will attack your protagonist, or the character with a phobia of creepy, crawly things will be plunged into a pit of creepy, crawly things. But just because an event will be inevitable, based on how you set things up, it doesn't mean you can't add your own twist or surprise to catch your reader off guard.

Because suspense results from tension being drawn out, you can look at an individual scene to analyze where you can either escalate things to a breaking point, or where you can twist the reader's expectation of what will happen.

Start by breaking up your scene into beats. Each action/response is a beat. For every action, ask yourself what your character hears, sees, smells, feels, tastes, or intuits. For every response, ask yourself how this is a degree higher in anxiety, dread, fear, or other kind of emotion. In other words, as incidents happen throughout the scene, how do they make things worse, emotionally, for your character? Is your character responding in an appropriately emotional way that shows us they're freaking out, worried, or on edge?

Because of that character–reader bond, the emotions your character experiences should also be emotions your reader experiences. Continuously ask yourself what you want your reader to be feeling in any given scene. This will help you set the scene up in a way that provokes the desired reader emotion. (This works for all kinds of emotions, not just suspense.)

If you hit a place in your scene where the action beat isn't worse or more tense than the beat before it, see if you can escalate the tension or decide if that's a good place where you can pivot the scene to take it in an unexpected direction.

DISCOVERY WORK

This exercise is helpful at any stage of the writing process, whether you're dealing with Draft 0 or Draft 14. It's also a marvelous exercise to help you bust through writer's block.

Pick a scene where you want to amplify the suspense. Whatever you choose, make sure there is something at stake for your character. They must accomplish this mission successfully or else.

Brainstorm some "*What if?*" statements to explore different ways to hinder your character on this mission. Analyze your action and response beats to make sure things are escalating appropriately.

What is your character feeling throughout this scene, and how is their emotion tightening or escalating?

Your suspense can be made even more dramatic if your character responds to an obstacle in such a way that creates more trouble for them. Or if they respond in a way that is a direct reflection of their flawed belief.

For example, the soccer player who suffers self-doubt about their athletic ability might fake an injury just to avoid a tough game.

Think about things that you as the author know about your scene but would be impossible for your character to know.

For example, they run for a door hoping to escape the house and avoid being caught by the enemy, but they end up in a broom closet. How can you set things up so that your character gets into deeper and deeper trouble?

25

Tone & Mood

All writing carries a particular attitude and feeling, and these can change depending on particular elements at play. When we roll out a piece of writing—be it a passage of exposition, a scene, or a dialogue exchange—tone and mood are expressed all the way down to the word-level. In every moment in a story. Writers need to ask themselves what attitude and feeling they intend to evoke in any given story moment, and why that particular tone and mood matters.

TONE

There are places and people and experiences in our lives that we perceive with a certain attitude. A victim of bullying might have an attitude of fearfulness toward school, a boy who grew up with a silver spoon in his mouth might have an attitude of arrogance toward those beneath him, a woman in love might have an attitude of passion toward her significant other.

As a kid, I spent many a summer on Cape Cod with my family. Of all the things we'd do, I think I loved going to the beach the most. My grandmother, Nanny, was a sun worshiper—she'd even get tanned in between her toes! I used to stretch out beside her, on my towel, thinking somehow I'd be blessed with the same glow. Sooner or later, though, my sister would urge me from my futile pursuit of golden skin and instead hunt for crabs in tide pools, climb jetties, or get a treat from the ice cream truck. To this day, whenever I hear the cry of seagulls, I'm transported back in time when salt and sand ranked right up there with chocolate, and play was a full-time job.

In the above passage, I've set the tone by conveying some sensory images, emotions, and information. With this tone established, you (or any reader) can easily sense my baseline attitude toward the beach, my family, and my childhood.

Tone can change, however. When a character goes through changes themselves, then their attitude toward things might change, as well. Or experiences with something might change with the passage of time or with the introduction of new people or situations. For example, a character might have loved school—until their family moved to a different town and the new school was so terrible that the character's attitude toward school switched from positive to negative. A character could have an attitude of nostalgia and comfort toward the beach because of their safe and happy experiences as a child. But what if one of their best friends from high school drowns in the ocean one summer? How then would your character's attitude toward the beach change? What kind of tone would they express when thinking about it? Their attitude would be much more complicated, a combination of happiness and grief.

Tone is expressed through a character's perception of any given situation, and it can change on a dime. When my daughter was applying for jobs, she described the process with an attitude of anxiety and annoyance. All the searching online. All the cover letters she had to write. All the different applications she had to fill out. When she got a call back from a potential employer, her tone shifted to hopefulness and excitement. The anxiety was still there, but it was a different kind of anxiety. It went from "When will someone call me back?" to "What if I don't get this job?"

A few examples of tone:

Sassy, joyful, desperate, close-minded, encouraging, clueless, defiant, confident, hypocritical, relaxed, goofy, indifferent, know-it-all, arrogant, sarcastic, playful, lighthearted, nostalgic, preachy, melodramatic, inspiring.

Word choice helps to convey tone, which in turn helps us get to know more about a character or a particular subject. A character who describes a blind date as "adventurous" gives us a completely different picture compared to one who describes a blind date as "a waste of time."

When you're deciding on tone, it's helpful to ask yourself who the viewpoint character or narrator is in the story moment. How do they feel about the subject at hand? Are they dreading the upcoming football game? Do they respect their boss? Do they agree with their friend's choice? Are they comfortable at the party?

Your story's genre might have one overall tone, such as a passionate romance or a sinister psychological thriller or a goofy comedy, but your narrator or viewpoint character may regard a particular subject in a different tone from the story's tone overall. For example, your historical romance may have an overall tone of passion, but your main character might spend a chapter here and there regarding love with a tone of wistfulness or detachment. That's okay as long as the tone fits the circumstances on the page and makes sense to the character's personality and experience at that moment.

While tone can shift because a character's attitude about a subject can shift, you want to make sure it's a plausible shift and there's a good reason for it. Too many inexplicable or unfounded changes in your character's attitude will make for a choppy reading experience. Maybe you're going for a tone of bubbly giddiness in your romantic comedy. But if you have a large number of scenes where the main character's tone is cold or indifferent, then that will impact the overall tone of your story.

MOOD

Tone and mood can be confused as one and the same thing, but they serve two different functions. Where tone is the viewpoint character's attitude toward a specific subject, mood is the atmosphere of the scene which a reader can feel or sense.

Part of the reason for the confusion between the two is because the same adjectives can be used to describe both elements. You can have a lighthearted tone to your novel, and the mood in a chapter can be lighthearted. You can have a sinister tone to your novel, and the mood in a chapter can also be sinister.

Because mood is about the vibe of what's happening on the page, that can be relayed through storytelling elements such as setting description, sensory details, showing versus telling, and imagery. A character walking through a dark forest might have an attitude of foreboding because they associate forests with danger. To support this tone so that the reader can feel that foreboding vibe, you would want to describe the forest as spooky, ominous, creepy. Sensory details such as rustles in the underbrush, the chilling breeze from a bird soaring too close, or smells of something rotting all add to the mood of fear, danger, and death.

However, mood doesn't always have to support the tone. Using the same dark forest above, let's play with mood. Your character could still have an attitude of foreboding, but the atmosphere of the forest could work to dispute that attitude. The rustles in the underbrush are squirrels playing chase. The birds flying too close are carrying nesting material or food for their young. The smells are of pine sap and freshly fallen leaves. These particular sensory details and images evoke a much different mood—one of comfort, playfulness, and life.

The functions of tone and mood depend on what you need to accomplish in your story moment and how that will impact the story and your character's arc overall. A character's attitude of foreboding regarding a dark forest works better if there's a reason behind it. Otherwise, you run into a problem of writing a cliché or setting something up and never paying it off. Adding the foreboding mood helps to bring the reader directly into the character's personal experience. Heck, yeah—if I'm walking through a dark forest and I hear rustling at my feet, I'm going to feel a little on edge, too. We bond with the character through the vibe of the scene.

But when we switch the mood to something nonthreatening that counters the character's attitude, something interesting happens. The playful and comfortable mood allows us to see how the character's attitude is keeping them shackled to their ghost and trapped in their weaknesses or flawed belief—preventing them from seeing things from a different perspective. The contrast between attitude and mood can also act as foreshadow to their eventual character transformation.

DISCOVERY WORK

1.| For the following list of places, describe each one using a positive tone, and then describe it using a negative tone.

Treehouse
Nightclub
Kitchen
Castle
Film studio
Circus
Science lab
Baseball field
Library
Sorcerer's den
Misty meadow

2.| Pick one of the places above and write a scene where mood contradicts the tone. How and why does this mood change in a subsequent scene?

26

Voice & Style

Whether you know it or not, you have voice and style! All writers do. Voice and style are part of your writer self. The trick is identifying and strengthening them. Out of anything in the craft, honing these two major storytelling elements might be the most complicated because they're so abstract and elusive. Don't fret if you have no clue what your voice and style are right now. You can figure them out with time and practice.

When you write, you're pulling from a place deep inside you, unconsciously making choices about how your story comes across to readers. These choices are pretty much intuitive, and that's where you're going to find your authentic voice and style.

Even though voice and style are already within you, they can be shaped and refined based on your personal preferences. For example, if you long to be known for having a witty and charismatic voice, but your writing sounds solemn, you can change it!

These two storytelling elements make up your writer identity, and it's important to have a handle on how they work and sound so that you can be sure you're using them to their greatest advantage. Let's dive a little deeper into the definitions of each one.

VOICE

This is probably the most obscure element in storytelling. Explaining voice is like explaining the smell of rain—you really don't know until you know. Until you experience the smell of rain for yourself.

If you were to Google the definition of "voice" in literature, you'll likely find many references that describe voice as the author's style. To me, that's a head scratcher. If voice is style, then what is style? True, there is overlap, but they aren't one and the same. So, I figured I'd give the definition a whirl, as I understand it.

Voice is the author's soul on the page, who they are at their core, which gives their writing a specific personality. Voice reflects the author's view of and experience with the world and everything in it. An author's voice isn't the same as the characters' voices. Rather, an author's voice is a distinctive, original sound that carries a story from beginning to end, often delivered via the narrator. Voice is an impression that an author leaves with their reader, something that the reader can use to identify the author simply by reading random pages.

Take singers or musicians as an example. You only have to hear a few words being sung by someone like Whitney Houston, Frank Sinatra, Adele, Bob Dylan, or Janis Joplin to know who's coming through the speaker.

Now, you're probably thinking that this sounds an awful lot like tone (chapter twenty-five), and I'll admit, the overlap is extreme. In fact, tone and voice are so similar that it's probably okay to treat them as one and the same in the beginning stages of your writing journey. (There are only so many balls you can juggle as you learn the craft!) However, I do think, to a point, tone is story-specific and voice is author-specific.

Have you ever been told to "Watch your tone!" by another? Or have you ever been in a discussion with someone where the words were tame, but the tone (the attitude) conveyed aggravation or accusation? Where the person spoke with their usual voice or personality—the core of who they are—it was the tone that gave away what they really thought or believed.

Tone is more apt to change depending on circumstances, where voice tends to be a constant because it's rooted in a deeper sense of self.

This isn't to say that voice can't ever change, but think about it like this: If voice is your soul or personality on the page, then the change has to be fundamental. It has to come from a change in deep-seated values or beliefs—and that requires some evolution. Voice doesn't change with the winds, and it doesn't go back and forth for no good reason. Tone is more flexible because it's situational and temporal—an attitude based on a person's opinion, mood, or circumstances.

It's a slight difference, yes, which is why I think you won't hurt your writing journey if you don't nail that down right away.

STYLE

Like voice, style is another impression an author leaves in their work, and it's something that a reader will expect from them. This doesn't just mean subject matter. It covers all the bases. From genre to POV to narrative tense to setting to character to dialogue to conflict to sentence construction to word choice—authors tend to write with a certain style that earmarks their scope of work.

Stephen King is not only known for his horror stories, but he often writes characters whose vocation is writing. Ernest Hemingway was known for his simple, minimalist writing, whereas Emily Brontë was known for her lyrical and poetic prose. J.R.R. Tolkien, George R.R. Martin, and J.K. Rowling are famous for their immersive and unique world-building.

Style is so personal that you could assign twenty different writers the same story premise—a teenaged boy who learns his father came from another universe with the mission to destroy Earth—and you would get twenty wildly different stories. This is because style is evident through all storytelling elements, from genre down to punctuation.

Writers who are just starting out tend to make unconscious choices in their stories via personal habits, lack of training, or even emulating their favorite authors. For instance, someone who envisions nature with an eye for detail might describe a setting with a lot of sensory images. A writer's male characters might sound tough, hard-to-read, or emotionally reserved because that's the writer's general experience with men. A person might tend to ramble in real life, so their sentences in a story might be overly long and complex. Someone who is an avid fan of *Little Women* might subconsciously write a story eerily similar in its cast of characters, story conflict, and setting.

Some of your unconscious choices may be beneficial to your story, and others not so much. Honing your personal writing style takes time and practice. It's an element that I wouldn't necessarily worry about if you're just starting out (again, too many balls to juggle!), but it is something you can examine and shape through journaling exercises.

DISCOVERY WORK

Because voice and style are an inherent part of your writing self, you should first work to identify what they look like or sound like on the page before you even consider shaping, modifying, fixing, or shaking things up at all.

A great place to start is any kind of journaling or writing that you've already done. It's probably safe to say you weren't paying attention to voice or style in these pieces (unless you've been trained in writing), so they'll be authentic. Read them out loud and let the cadence, flow, mood, tone, sentence construction, word choice, and worldview just sink in. If you want to make notes of your initial takeaways, go for it. Try not to judge. Simply observe.

Next, select some of your favorite books from your favorite authors. Study their voices and styles. What do you love? What inspires you? If you could emulate anything, what would it be? This isn't plagiarizing or copying—I'm not suggesting you strive to be C.S. Lewis 2.0. But we all have literary heroes and heroines. We all fell in love with writing because we once read a book that stayed with us long after we reached THE END. Authors inspired us to be authors. There's no shame or guilt in figuring out what kind of writer you'd like to be based on writers that you've admired.

Once you've begun to get a feel for your personal style preferences and your writing voice, you can play around in your secret garden of writing. If you have some fiction already underway, take a random page—just for fun—and mess around with the voice and style. Don't hold back from experimenting. Be bold. Nothing is set in stone. Your secret garden is risk-free but full of opportunity and revelations.

PART THREE

JOURNEY WITH YOUR MUSE

JOURNEY WITH YOUR MUSE

Welcome to the final section of the book, where we talk about the journey ahead for you and your Muse.

Unless you're writing for your own pleasure and aren't keen on finding an audience or selling your books, be prepared for a difficult writing journey. But it can be a rewarding one, too!

If you're brand new to the gig, allow for a period of learning and skill-building where you write just to write, letting the experience be self-indulgent, fun, and pressure-free. You'll eventually reach a point in your writing process where you'll be ready to make the pivot to "writing for real" as I touched upon in chapter seven.

If you're someone who's traveled back and forth across the writing terrain, then you likely sport some battle scars. You may even be tired or disillusioned. The idea of writing for fun is harder to accept. But you're not quite ready to give up either, so you're willing to get back to the basics, take some refresher courses, and try again.

Or maybe you're somewhere in between. You've written stories, but you don't call yourself an experienced writer—or perhaps you struggle with calling yourself a writer, period. You know there's stuff you still need to learn, and aspects of yourself that still need to grow.

The common denominator among all of the above is the call to write.

And every writer's call is a personal one that needs to be shaped via that writer's natural writing forces.

Writers are meant to thrive in their journeys, but as writers travel deeper, they encounter more challenges and tougher tests. Many of these obstacles have nothing to do with flaws in their works-in-progress, but rather are thrown at them by Life. You'll be forced to make decisions (many difficult decisions) that align with your dream to write and publish stories.

This next section covers some examples of situations you might encounter throughout your writing journey and provides strategies to help you navigate possible emotional and mental pitfalls.

So, get ready as we learn ways to push forward on a journey with your Muse so that you can weather the long game of writing in a way that leads you into your best version of a Transformed Writer.

27

Your Purpose

When my daughter Maddy was around eleven years old, she tried out for our town's swim team and after a few days of trials, she made it. She was so excited. The team is a big deal with strict rules, high expectations, and a nine-month commitment.

The team practiced at the local pool most afternoons, and on Friday nights, they practiced at the University of New Hampshire, about a fifteen-minute drive from home. Competitions were held almost every weekend, and they tended to be an all-day affair.

Being one of the newer swimmers, Maddy wasn't scheduled for out-of-state competitions immediately, so she settled into the team and the rigorous practice schedule fairly easily.

But once she was scheduled for some meets, things got stressful fast. She was required to go to more practices and to stay longer. Her coach critiqued her more often, assigning her to all sorts of races that she didn't feel confident about.

The pressure was on.

Maddy began to struggle with nerves. She still loved the sport, but the competition was fierce, and it got to her head. She was on a losing streak, and she lost all confidence. Three months in, she wanted to quit.

As a mom, I was conflicted. Do I let her quit based on her belief that she wasn't good enough to compete? Or do I make her tough it out?

When one of her friends dropped out of the team for similar low-confidence reasons, Maddy's desire to quit increased tenfold.

I made the difficult decision to tell her she couldn't. I explained that she'd made a commitment to the team for nine months and she needed to see it through. After the season, if she still wanted to drop out, then she could.

Needless to say, she wasn't happy with me.

My fear was that I'd be sending a damaging message if I let her quit just because winning wasn't easy. That she didn't have what it takes to push through the tough challenges.

To Maddy's credit, she continued to work hard. She went to all the practices and put forth her best effort. She could have defied me and simply stopped trying, but she didn't. She persevered and showed up, day after day, even though it was tough.

Several meets came and went without her winning a single heat, and I started doubting my decision. What if I'm making things worse by forcing her to stick with it? What if things go completely sideways, and she comes out of this thing losing faith in herself entirely?

Then, at the end of seven months, at a meet in New York, she won her first heat. The look on her face was a mixture of pure shock and incredible joy. All the work she'd invested finally paid off, and she saw the light at the end of the tunnel.

For the next couple of months, she won some more heats and consistently improved her times. She ended the season on a high note, having grown into a stronger, more skilled swimmer than she was when she'd first joined the team.

The obvious takeaway here is that if I'd allowed her to quit, then she never would have experienced this amazing win. She never would have learned what she's capable of and that she's stronger than she thought.

True, her win came as a result of sacrifice—but what win doesn't?

The journey toward any goal often has a stretch where we lose faith in ourselves because it's filled with obstacles and challenges. If a goal is easily attained, without a single thing blocking our way, then we won't learn much about our potential. We'll miss out on learning what we're capable of, how strong we really are. (Sounds awfully like character development, doesn't it?)

At some point in your writing journey, things will get tough. So tough that you'll experience self-doubt. You might even lose faith in yourself and start thinking you're not worthy of being a writer because the wins are few and far between.

Giving up is an option, of course. However, I recommend thinking long and hard about your reason for giving up. If you give up because you don't think you're good enough, then you risk damaging your self-worth. It'll be much more difficult to return to the journey, not to mention trying anything new.

You *always* have a choice. Every single day that you pursue your Audacious Dream, you have a choice about how you'll handle that day. You may have a list of tasks you want to accomplish; write a certain number of words; vent to a writer-friend; or take a day off from your WIP.

Whatever you choose to do, it helps to know why you're doing it, even down to the smallest task, as this maintains an open line of communication with your Muse and keeps you on a path you want to be on.

In truth, your "why" is the strongest weapon you can wield.

Notice how this is similar to the way we move our fictional characters along the plot of their story. Their actions are stronger and more believable when they're backed by their personal "why." Even the smallest choices matter to their grander story goal.

Your "why," also known as your purpose, is what sustains you. This motivation drives you in everything you do. The clearer you are on your "why," the more empowered you'll feel on your journey.

Writing journeys thoroughly test their adventurers, but when the gremlins come knocking, you can lean into your "why" to help you overcome them.

When you think about your "why," you'll automatically tap into your natural writing forces, specifically your values. Who do you want to be on this journey? What values are important for you to uphold during this journey?

Purpose and values often work together. Where purpose gives you a target to shoot for, your values are the daily principles that keep you on track, internally, toward your purpose.

As a writer, your Audacious Dream may be to become a #1 New York Times bestselling author. Maybe you have a desire to share your story about rising from homelessness, and perhaps you want to donate 10 percent of all sales to homeless veterans. Your values of social responsibility and empathy for others in need are what keep you on this path.

It's not unusual for purpose to change as progress is made along the journey. It's also not unusual to have more than one purpose. Experiences, relationships, and lessons learned along the way shape and transform people. With growth comes new ideas, a new way of looking at ourselves, and a new way of seeing our potential.

Goals are an important part of your writing life, because they encourage you to strive to do bigger and better things. Goals encourage you to improve yourself and to seek happiness and fulfillment.

However, goals have a way of stealing the spotlight, especially when they're the audacious kind. Not only do they narrow your focus, but they can sometimes make you feel like you have no business trying to attain them.

Goals shouldn't be the thing you need in your life to feel complete. Rather, your true focus should be on your purpose and values. Who you want to be from one day to the next, knowing that whoever you are today will impact who you will be tomorrow.

Your journey will lead you to the writer you want to become. And to "become" anything, you have to go through tests and challenges.

Just like the heroes and heroines we write about.

DISCOVERY WORK

1.| Explore your purpose: Why do you want to be a writer? How will it enrich your overall life? How will your writing impact others? Where do you see yourself in three, ten, twenty years? What do you want your life to be all about? Who do you want to be in your creative journey? What is at stake if you can't fulfill your purpose?

2.| Explore your values: What messages do you have to share with the world? What is important to you and why is it important for you to share those values? How will you share your values? What is at stake if you can't share your values with others?

3.| When things are feeling so shaky that giving up is a consideration, take a time-out from your work for a minimum of three weeks. When you're feeling more refreshed, try any of these suggestions:

- Evaluate your natural writing forces and flag anything that doesn't feel good to you. Decide how you can make some changes.

- Join (or switch to) a new writing group.

- Hire a coach (or change coaches).

- Stow your current WIP and start a different project.

- Sometimes, setting a deadline is useful, as it was for me when making the decision about my daughter. We signed up for a certain time commitment with the swim team, and I used that to explain to her the importance of honoring your commitments, which is a life skill, anyway. Look at a calendar and decide on an end-date where you'll wrap things up if you still aren't happy.

- Call a friend! Talk to someone who's familiar with you and with your journey, someone you can talk to without fear of judgment. This person will see things from a different perspective and help you think beyond your limiting beliefs.

- Read books! All kinds of books. Read your old faithfuls and try new genres and new authors. Read for pleasure, but also read with a writer's eye. See if inspiration or motivation stirs within you.

- Start a blog about your writing struggles. You might be surprised how many people will comment with similar troubles. It's a marvelous way to make connections and you won't feel so alone.

- Make sure you haven't set unfair expectations for yourself. An Audacious Dream isn't accomplished overnight, or in a short span of time, or easily! The more Audacious the Dream, the more challenging the journey.

28

Bust Through Writer's Block

When I was a teenager, I didn't know what writer's block was. I mean, I understood what it was, I had just never personally experienced it. Creativity had always come easy. It knew no bounds, and I never shied away from the idea of the outlandish, improbable, far-fetched, or magical.

All of those concepts only pushed me onward.

Then I grew up.

Suddenly, the world was limiting, scary, judgmental.

And writer's block became a part of that world.

There are plenty of people out there who insist that writer's block isn't real, and that writers made up the concept to dramatize their creative lives. These same people might say, "You don't hear a doctor claiming she has doctor's block, or a teacher claiming he has teacher's block."

I can understand that point of view. However, writer's block is a label. It's just another way of saying, "I'm stuck on this idea, and I don't know how to work through it."

Writers may have unwittingly victimized themselves by personalizing what is actually an issue that all humans, regardless of career or hobby, deal with at one time or another.

Writer's block is a real issue (being unsure about what to do next), but it doesn't have to be something we dread. It doesn't have to grab us by the throat and hold us hostage.

The top two causes of writer's block:

- Lack of information

- Fear

LACK OF INFORMATION

This basically means that something isn't working in your story, but you don't know what it is or why it isn't working. It could be anything from character motivation to stakes to plausibility. It's important to remember that even though you may be blocked in the middle of your book—say, chapter twenty-eight—that the *root of the problem* isn't necessarily in chapter twenty-eight. In fact, and you need to take a deep breath here, it's extremely possible that the root of the problem could go all the way back to your early story-building notes.

I've seen writers hack and hack and hack at a single chapter because that's where they got stuck. The problem with this approach is that it's too narrow and doesn't factor in possible foundational issues. It's like sticking a poster over a crack in the wall. They're only dealing with the symptom, not the root cause.

Research is the best antidote to lack of information. Research can help you stay in proactive, problem-solving mode with your story, which can prevent the writer's block from feeling too overwhelming or getting worse.

GENERAL RESEARCH

Remember those open-ended questions from chapter two? *Why? Why not? What if . . . ?* Well, those are the kinds of questions you want to ask yourself when you're dealing with writer's block. What do I need to happen next? What precipitated this event? How should my character react? How can I escalate the stakes? What kind of reaction do I want from my reader? (Get as specific as possible, depending on what's going on with your story.)

Write down all possible solutions or answers to your questions. (A marvelous prompt to help you dig deeper is to follow up each of your responses with "Yes, and . . . ") Highlight the ones that get you excited. Basically, you're back in discovery mode, but that's okay. This is a stage you'll need to dip into throughout the writing process.

After exploring, test the ideas that you highlighted before diving back into your draft and making changes. Make sure the idea not only works for the spot where you were blocked, but that it's a plausible idea that adds dramatic tension to your whole story.

SPECIFIC RESEARCH

Character: What is your viewpoint character's motivation for anything they do in the chapter? The most common question I ask my writing clients is "Why" or "Why not?" when it comes to analyzing a character's actions. Be sure you're clear on why they do the things they do and why they respond to situations in a certain way. Then test their motivation against the story events for plausibility and dramatic tension. Be sure you're putting *all* your antagonists to work! Who can show up to give your protagonist a hard time? Who can switch sides and cause even more mayhem?

Setting: Settings often dictate how a scene unfolds or progresses. Are you using your setting to its full advantage? The wrong locale can restrict your characters, lower the stakes, or water down the tension. Even the sense of time you're using could slow your pace, or be an inappropriate fit for the mood you want to create. What do you *not* know about your setting that could be useful to your story?

Conflict and Stakes: Make sure that your character's situation is at a low point that highlights or increases the stakes. Are things getting worse for your character, or are they still in the same pot of boiling water? What if you raise the temperature? What if you add another problem? Sometimes, we get stuck in a scene because it isn't going anywhere. It's flaccid and dull, and we're burying ourselves with the weight of sluggish material. Injecting more conflict and raising the stakes can sometimes help you wiggle out of the corner you're boxed in.

Plot: Do you have a clear cause-and-effect trail of events? Go back a couple chapters prior to where you're stuck and mark the most major "cause" you can find. From there, mark all subsequent effects> causes > effects until you reach the point where you're stuck. Trace the entire line of plot. Is it plausible? Are you missing steps? What are the stakes? Is there tension throughout and is it escalating? What if you change something in a preceding chapter—would that help you in this one?

You can also examine the plot by marking the cause-and-effect trail going forward from the point where you're stuck. Ask yourself the same questions above. You're looking for plausibility and dramatic tension and stakes. What if you increased the tension in either the cause or effect at the point where you're blocked?

FEAR

This basically means you're allowing yourself to fight, flee, or freeze over something to do with your writing journey. This could include the specific story you're working on, pressure you're feeling from the journey itself, negative reviews of your work, limiting beliefs about your ability, the publishing process, etc.

Fear is a crafty little gremlin that comes in many disguises. Procrastination, lack of time, disruptions, loss of motivation, lack of ideas, illness . . . the list goes on. Fear creates writer's block because your subconscious has hooked into the limiting belief of "I can't XYZ." This is fear, all dressed up and everywhere to haunt.

Combating fear so that it doesn't inter*fear* with your creativity requires some practice with mindset. I touch on mindset a lot in Part One of this book. Basically, you want to lift yourself up from low points by repeating positive "I can . . . " or "I have the potential to . . . " statements and take action steps based on those statements.

Self-talk leads us to the next logical action step. When our self-talk is negative, then our next logical action step is rooted in negativity. We're more likely to limit or stifle ourselves because of what we believe about our abilities or skills.

On the other hand, when our self-talk is positive, we're more likely to take positive action steps that move us forward and help us evolve. You don't have to take enormous steps. The smallest positive step is magical enough to help you see your potential.

Moving forward means we're busting through writer's block and other nefarious traps set by fear. Our mindset work doesn't stop once we bust through any of these traps, though. Mindset work is a daily practice, and if fear is sneaking its way in and holding you hostage, you need to strengthen this practice.

One of my daily mantras for boosting creativity is: "Yes, and . . . " (Note that this is a handy prompt for story development, also.) This expression puts me in the mindset of possibility no matter what I'm up against. This works even when I'm in a trouble spot. When I spiral into "No,

I can't" or "I'm so bad at this" territory, I pivot as early as possible.

I might flail and crash about, get irritated or discouraged because writing is hard, and sometimes I wonder what the hell I think I'm doing here. But I'll try to catch myself in the midst of that, calm down, and make my pivot. It might go like this: "Okay, so, I'm stuck. This chapter is kicking my ass right now. Can I figure out a better way? Yes, and . . . "

From there, I list out as many seeds of ideas that my Muse delivers to me. **This pivot spins me away from the confining claws of fear and into the empowering gears of research.** By simply asking myself questions that allow for possibility and option and choice, I'm choosing a path that puts me in an empowered position with my story.

Writer's block is busted the minute we see options with our story. Even though we may discover there's a major foundational flaw in it, we have vision and we have possibility. We're more informed, and this is empowering.

DISCOVERY WORK

Writer's block can happen when your creative well isn't filled with enough ideas, creative energy, or inspiration. This lack can lead to self-doubt and fear. While it's easy to allow yourself to get caught up in this storm of negative thinking, you have the power to shift your mind into a more positive space.

Below are two tricks you can use to disrupt the storm of negativity:

1. Spend your day learning or trying something new.

2. Spend your day enjoying an old favorite pastime or revisit a favorite haunt.

Both of these options stir the well of your creativity, breathing life and energy into what has become stagnant.

If you choose to learn or try something new, you're filling your creative well with adventure and discovery. You're challenging your mind and spirit with new information and new experiences. Risk-taking is exciting and expands the boundaries of your comfort zone. You automatically grow from doing something different, and this growth spills over into your creative life because you now have new information, new details, new experiences, and new awareness to draw from.

If you opt to enjoy an old favorite pastime or revisit a favorite haunt, then you're filling your creative well with comfort and familiarity. You're connecting to your conscience, your heart, and your soul. You're taking time away from the pressures of performing and reminding yourself that creativity and inspiration come in many forms. You're also reminding yourself of the things in your life that you already have or the experiences you've already enjoyed that can help prove that some of the best secrets are hidden right beneath your nose.

29

Revising Draft 0

Imagine you're movin' and groovin' along Draft 0 when you start to wonder if your Inciting Incident is strong enough. You're already nearing the point of the Big Battle: Do you stop everything and go back to check? Or imagine you've been wrangling a chapter that doesn't feel interesting or compelling: Do you continue hacking away at it, or do you leave it and move on? Or imagine your predetermined finish line is fifty thousand words, but you can't seem to get past twenty thousand words before the whole story falls apart, so you keep starting over.

All these scenarios are real-world examples from writers I've worked with over the years. (There are plenty more where those came from.) Revision is the beast that lurks in the corner of your writing habitat, straining against its chain, desperate to get its paws on your manuscript because it's so sure it knows what to do, all the time.

Depending on what kind of story you're dealing with—and your experience level as a writer and your natural writing forces—you may or may not know how to deal with revision.

I personally adore revision. Yes, it's still a beast that lurks in my writing habitat, but I've learned how to tame it so that we co-create on my terms.

But revision isn't always easy to manage, so I want to chat about potential traps you might encounter and how to deal with them.

REVISING WHILE WRITING

At some point while you're writing Draft 0, you may be tempted to revise a portion of your story before you've reached your predetermined finish line. For instance, your story may have lost steam in the middle because your character made a decision that was too low-stakes. Or you may have written yourself into a corner where the event you're currently trying to write is inconsistent with the logical flow of those preceding it (otherwise known as a plot hole).

While those are major issues, you need to ask yourself if taking a time-out to revise will help you continue onward. It really depends on your natural writing forces. Disrupting your writing flow can slow your momentum. It can also give you the message to not trust your initial story ideas. On the flip side, revising your early writing before you have a full draft can provide a clearer view of the path ahead, and it could boost your confidence. Sometimes, revision can feel easier or more manageable than brand-new writing, and this can be a good way to keep your hands in the manuscript even though you're not churning out new material. Again—how do you work best?

If you want to revise portions of Draft 0 before a full draft is complete, my advice is to put a time limit or session limit on the revisions. This allows you to get in and out of revision quickly and back to the main objective, which is to complete your draft.

If you choose to push onward, leave yourself notes along the way. You can insert them directly in your content (use a colored font and a special icon as a placeholder for easy search and find), in the margins (using track changes in MS Word or comments in Google Docs), or in a separate notebook.

REVISING REPEATEDLY

The revision loop is easy to jump on, but difficult to exit. Revision can feel good because you think you're cleaning up a big ol' mess and this will help the rest of your manuscript shine. However, if you're revising an incomplete draft, then you're only spot-cleaning because you don't know how the rest of the story plays out. Allow yourself one revision per scene and move onward. Another option is to leave yourself author notes in the margins where you see potential issues, and this can be a useful, short-term substitute for revision.

REVISING TOO QUICKLY

You've reached your personal finish line—hurrah!—and you're eager to get cracking on it, so you start rewriting immediately. I urge you to take a break for a minimum of two weeks. Put it somewhere you can't see it or pick at it. Use the break to fill your creative well in other ways or bone up on the craft. It's easier to be objective about how to revise your work after you've taken time away.

GETTING FEEDBACK TOO EARLY

Unless you're working with an experienced writing coach or editor, I caution you against seeking feedback on Draft 0. These are your rough ideas, and they aren't ready for the catwalk quite yet. You'll either receive bland comments like "This is nice" or "I like your main character," or you'll get stinging criticism that sears doubt into your mind about your story.

Wait until you've completed Draft 0 and you've put it away for a two-week minimum. Then, pull out the manuscript and read it through, jotting notes in the margins or in a notebook. Try not to make changes yet—just read and observe. This gentle reintroduction to your story will help you see any issues with a clearer eye and an open mind.

At this point, you might want to run your early draft by someone else who can help you with next-step decisions. Writing partners, writing groups, coaches, or editors are all possible choices. Who you choose to work with depends on a number of factors. However, you may decide you want to keep going on your own and try your hand at the next draft by yourself, with no outside influence. There is no wrong route here—only the route that feels good to you.

It's helpful to set boundaries when you're up against the question of revision. Understand who you are as a writer and whether you're someone who might need to do some rewriting during the writing process. What will that look like for you? Why do you need to rewrite before Draft 0 is complete?

The revision process itself, post Draft 0, is also best determined by your natural writing forces. I generally advise writers to deal with the big-picture elements first (just like I do when writers are embarking on a new story), and then work their way down from there. But again, every story and every writer is different, so you need to figure out the conditions under which revision will work best for you.

DISCOVERY WORK

Revision isn't just about fine-tuning the manuscript. It's also about understanding your story from a more evolved perspective. If you try to revise your manuscript as the same writer who wrote that draft, you won't be able to see the changes you need to make, much less be able or willing to make those changes.

This is one of the reasons why I recommend spending some time away from a finished draft. After a couple of weeks, without looking at that draft, journal through what kind of story you intended to write. Go back to chapter eight of this book (Getting To Know Your Story) and answer those discovery questions again. You may find that your answers are somewhat different now that you've completed your manuscript, and this is absolutely normal. It's also telling. It means you've grown a little bit and learned something new about your story (or yourself) that makes a difference in how you want to approach your next steps.

After you've done some journaling on your purpose and your vision for the story you want to tell, you're ready to look at that draft. It's best if you can read the whole draft in one sitting with minimal disruptions, as that approach will keep the material fresh in your head. If you need several days, then make notes in a separate document or notebook to help keep track of storylines, characters, and other elements.

You may want to print out your manuscript and mark up the pages with a pen or a highlighter. Or you may want to work on a computer and highlight passages or use the comment feature.

It's a good idea to first focus your attention on the big-picture elements like plotlines, structure, and character arcs. Smaller elements might stand out to you, such as dialogue or scene transitions, especially if you're a detail-oriented person, so flag those as necessary. Just keep in mind that smaller issues are likely by-products of larger issues.

As you read, you want to simultaneously track the story's progression and stay aware of your intentions and vision for your story. How do you feel when you're reading through your story? Not only are you looking for story-level issues, searching for what's currently not working in the story, but you also want to be mindful of how you can take this story to the next level. As I mentioned above, revision is more than fine-tuning a manuscript. Revision is an opportunity to improve your skills and elevate yourself as a writer.

While you're assessing the shape of your manuscript, continually ask yourself, "Is this story aligning with my vision and my intentions? What can I do to elevate the storytelling?"

Some questions to ask yourself to get started:

1.| What is the cause–effect in these plot events? What is the reason behind these events? Are these events plausible and do they escalate with tension?

2.| What is the motivation for Character X in this scene? Does that motivation need more setup or explanation for the reader to understand?

3.| What are the stakes in this scene?

4.| Why is Character X the viewpoint character in this scene? Would another character provide a more compelling lens? (For stories that have multiple viewpoint characters.)

5.| How does my setting express my characters and their goals or fears?

6.| How does my backstory add value to the forward-moving plot?

7.| What is the balance of showing versus telling in this scene and how does it impact the pace?

Obviously, these questions barely scratch the surface. Add your own questions as you go along and personalize them as you see fit. You may want to keep your answers to your questions in a separate document or notebook, or perhaps you want to make notes directly in the manuscript. Do what works best for you.

It may help to categorize all your notes by storytelling element (e.g., structure, character, plot, setting) so that you can see how those elements evolve from beginning to end.

After you compile all your notes, take time to make notes about your notes. Seriously. This relates to your intentions and vision for your book. What lights you up about your characters? What aspect(s) of your plot feels flat or disappointing? Which scenes drop the ball with reader expectation? Which scenes feel surprising and fresh? Where has your setting met your standards and where has it fallen short? In what ways does your story fit the genre and audience expectations? What do you need to do to take your story to the next level?

It may help to take another few days to let your feelings sink in about this current draft. If you're feeling wobbly, uncertain, anxious, or any other kind of negative, resistant emotion, please take time to shore up your mindset before you begin writing again. I really think that's important. Revision can be overwhelming and daunting, and it loves to kick a writer when they're already down. Get your mindset in a space that welcomes a challenge, that accepts the hard job that is revision, before you begin working on the next draft. You could also take this time to decide how you want to approach the work for your next draft.

Some writers like to start with the first page and work chapter-by-chapter, in order, referring to the big-picture notes along the way. Other writers might want to create an outline with their new ideas and changes before actively revising. Still, other writers might work on one storytelling element at a time, for instance, handling character development from beginning to end, then tackling plot from beginning to end, then dealing with theme from beginning to end, etc.

How you decide to go about revision depends on your natural writing forces. Work to your strengths. Whenever you struggle to the point where you slow down or halt altogether, reach out to another writer, an editor, or a coach to help you get back on track.

30

The Inner Critic

If you hear a voice in your head saying anything negative about your writing, that's an Inner Critic (IC). This is a normal companion on the writing journey, but that doesn't make the experience any less annoying—or damaging.

When my IC first showed up, it completely took over my thoughts, beliefs, and self-talk. My IC didn't just stick to criticizing my writing, it strove to sabotage all areas of my life. And because I was feeling vulnerable already, my writing came to a screeching halt. However, my desire to write (and enjoy the process) was such a strong force in my life, I knew I had to figure out how to kick my IC to the curb.

Unfortunately, I don't think it's possible to totally eradicate an Inner Critic, because believe it or not, it does serve a useful purpose (more on that below). However, ICs can be tamed so that the criticism is constructive, not damaging.

One of the first things I did was name my Inner Critic (Eris). Giving my IC its own personality was helpful to separate myself (and my writing) from the damaging messages. From there, I wrote Eris letters in my journal.

At first, I wasn't sure what to say, but I was clear on my ultimate objective: I needed to wrangle Eris to a point where we could co-create.

After a while, I realized why Eris showed up when I least needed her. She was my voice of fear, serving to protect me every time I stepped outside my comfort zone. She would reinforce my self-doubts about my talent or ability to write with simple but clear statements: "You're not good enough." "You can't do this." "You didn't win that writing contest, so that means you're not a good writer."

Ah, yes—do you recognize the sounds of a flawed belief system?

When I saw that I was living by the code of a flawed belief, I knew I needed to construct empowered beliefs that would serve me.

I was already journaling at this point, so it was easy enough for me to break down this belief system through lots of mindset exercises.

SELF-REFLECTION + ASSESSMENTS

I know it's difficult to be honest (and positive) with oneself, especially when things aren't going well. However, living by the code of a flawed belief will keep you stuck, spinning your wheels, and unfulfilled.

Change is hard, and it's scary. But change is necessary for growth. Sometimes, it's easier when we approach change slowly and with intention. That's why journaling is helpful. It serves as a tracking system and record-keeper of your emotions and goals as you motor along your writing journey. You can find patterns in your behavior and thoughts. You can also learn your natural writing forces and compare those over time or projects.

When you discover favorable traits, highlight them and look for ways that you can cement these into your daily creative life. You want to be operating from these beliefs and values as often as possible.

For those traits that hold you back, be careful not to judge yourself too harshly. (This includes anything associated with your Inner Critic.) We all have characteristics that block us from our true potential. We all get down on ourselves for one thing or another.

First, get clear on how or in what way these aspects create challenges for you. It's not enough to know you're a procrastinator—you need to understand how procrastination makes your writing life more difficult. Putting the trait into context enables you to take specific action steps to combat it.

Next, work on the messaging that surrounds these aspects. Changing a trait or a habit takes a lot of time and effort; however, flipping your self-talk in relation to this flaw takes seconds.

Once you reconstruct the self-talk from negative to positive, your next step is to incorporate that message throughout your days. After approximately three weeks of regularly leaning into your new positive statement (experts claim it can take about twenty-one days to establish a new habit), it'll become a strong enough presence that it begins to rival the original negative thought or behavior.

With enough perseverance on your part, that new positive thought could even become automatic.

Easier said than done—our Inner Critics are stubborn folk. Often, they've been a part of our lives since childhood or adolescence. As I mentioned above, I don't think you can oust your IC completely, but you can tame it, and the best way to do that is to reframe your IC's messaging.

CREATIVE HEALTH CHECK-UPS

Remember, your Muse is an inherent part of you, so it must be nurtured just like any other part of yourself. When you have a healthy relationship with your Muse, your overall creative life will thrive.

This isn't to say that your output has to be a constant flow or that ideas are flying in nonstop. It doesn't mean you should never experience rough patches or feel low on creative energy. This also doesn't suggest that your Inner Critic should never act out. But every writer has a tipping point, and if you ignore your personal warning signs for too long, your overall creative life will be negatively impacted.

Here again, you need to know your natural writing forces so that you can recognize your personal yellow and red flags. These could include avoiding a project, letting the real world interfere with a prescheduled writing session, experiencing writer's block, suffering from imposter syndrome—anything that is out of the norm or exacerbated is a sign you need to pivot.

Your Inner Critic isn't a villain out to get you. Its main job is to protect you. I actually think the IC is a modern-day version of our fight-flight-freeze mentality. Rather than being on the lookout for saber-toothed tigers, we have to watch our backs for rejections, failures, and humiliation. Our IC understands the boundaries of our personal comfort zone (Status-Quo World) and will do everything possible to keep us safe and secure.

Just like it's helpful to nurture a working relationship with your Muse, it's helpful to nurture a working relationship with your IC.

One way to do this is to write a letter to your IC to let it know you're gearing up to step outside your comfort zone. Explain that you're purposely taking a risk and that you're prepared for the consequences. This can help tone down the IC's knee-jerk reaction to protect you.

Creativity is always evolving, and so are you. What worked a year ago may not suffice today. A trait that held you back five years ago may not be present anymore. Life for you, outside of writing, may have changed drastically, and this may have impacted your creativity in ways you didn't anticipate.

Running self-assessments and creative check-ups will help you stay on track. To thrive in your creative life, you need to know what works, what doesn't work, and why. This includes building healthy relationships with your Muse and your Inner Critic so that you're living a prosperous, fulfilling, harmonious, and joyful creative life.

DISCOVERY WORK

Take your Inner Critic out to dinner. If you don't already have a name, a backstory, or a personality for your Inner Critic, this is a great time to find out all of that stuff. Bring a journal, sketchbook, pens, colored pencils, highlighters, and any other tool you think would be useful in this endeavor.

Ask your Inner Critic all kinds of questions about the reasons why they rise up and get in your way whenever you embark on a creative project. Listen to what they have to say so that you can respond with more questions. This isn't a time to argue. This is a time to understand, listen, and find a way to work with your Inner Critic.

Remember, your Inner Critic isn't a villain out to get you. Their main objective is to protect you. This means that you have to find a way to explain your goals and the reasons why those goals are important to you. When you can relay your intentions and your vision clearly to your Inner Critic, they'll give you more space and opportunity to take risks.

31

SEASONS OF STAGNATION

We don't start off as the writers we want to be. Point A of our journeys reflects the writers we are at the moment. The experiences we undergo—the positive and the negative—spur us from our Point A selves to the writers we want to become: Point X.

There's an opportunity for an arc of growth here, and this arc of growth will respond to the actions you take and the decisions you make. There will be many seasons where you feel like you're not growing, but stagnating (even flatlining, she mutters under her breath), and that's to be expected.

No. Not expected.

Embraced.

Sometimes, we must stay in the same place a while to allow the growth or the learning to truly sink in. We're just not ready to move forward or take the next step—for whatever reason. Think of it like treading water instead of swimming. You may not be going anywhere, physically, but you're maintaining, strengthening, and locking in the work you've already put in, and that's a different kind of forward progression.

These seasons of treading water can be over in a flash, or they may last years. Yeah, that's probably not great news to hear. I personally have endured several years-long periods of flatlin—er, stagnation, and the first couple of times sucked me so dry I gave up writing.

Looking back on those seasons, I now know what I did wrong. I put emphasis on the wrong aspect of my journey—all my eggs were in the destination basket, and none of them were in the journey basket.

You may have heard the advice that the real magic is in the journey, not the destination, and this is true for a number of reasons. One reason is because if we tend to the journey more intimately and with joy, we're less likely to worry about how long it's taking us to reach our destination.

The other big reason is because the journey is where the true character development happens. We're the heroes of our own stories. We go through an outer journey consisting of our writing endeavors and an inner journey where we grow and change as a result of the outer journey.

Those seasons of stagnation are necessary for internal growth. When things are relatively quiet or slow in our outer journeys, we should take the downtime to practice healthy mindset choices, build our skills, work with a story coach, join a writing group—basically, not freaking out about the fact that nothing seems to be happening and instead relishing the opportunity to connect even more deeply and strongly to our Muse.

Still, stagnation can be frustrating and irritating because you're not seeing external progress, so it feels like you're not getting any better as a writer. This feeling gets under your skin and triggers limiting beliefs. Stagnation is a breeding ground for procrastination, self-doubt, and thoughts of giving up. Your destination suddenly feels impossible to reach.

As I mentioned before, when you hit a low point, you should step back and self-reflect. Try to do this before all the limiting beliefs and self-doubt get the better of you. Remind yourself that you are on *a journey* and that means you have to experience setbacks and challenges because they spur growth.

DISCOVERY WORK

Look at the endpoints of both your outer journey (how your writing is developing) and your inner journey (how you are developing). Point A is where you started, both in your outer and inner journeys. Point X is your destination (again, both in your outer and inner journeys).

For both the outer and inner journeys, answer the following questions:

1.| What progress have you made since Point A? How does this progress make you feel? What have you sacrificed to make this progress?

2.| What have you learned about yourself and your writing so far?

3.| What else needs to happen between where you're at now and Point X?

4.| If there are action steps you can take, make a list of tasks you can reasonably do this week and work your way to the tasks that will need to be done farther out in time. If you can, pin dates or at least some kind of time frame to these tasks. Bonus points for scheduling tasks in your calendar.

5.| Describe how you're feeling about Point X. Has your viewpoint changed in any way from when you first started out? What does that mean to you?

6.| If you're in a season of stagnation, what activity can you do this month to improve your skills? Is there another writer in your life who you might be able to help out? Is there any specific mindset work you can hone for the next month or two?

32

Mapping Out Your Writing Journey

Writers are the heroes of their own creative journeys. A writer sets a dream goal for themselves and then needs to follow a path fraught with obstacles, setbacks, failures (and some wins!). As they push forward on their path, they encounter situations that help them grow skills, learn the ropes of the industry, overcome inner flaws that stand in their way, and battle any external antagonists that might make the journey more difficult.

Sometimes, the path a writer initially plots for themselves isn't doing the job, so they have to adjust. Make new decisions. Set smaller or different goals that they hadn't anticipated. Take a break. Ask for help. Try again.

Other times, the path is so horrendously challenging that a writer becomes disillusioned with the entire idea of writing a book, and they take a break or give up.

Whatever you choose to do, being true to yourself is the healthiest way to go. (A gentle reminder to get clear on your "why"—your purpose. What is your writing journey really about?)

In addition to being clear on your "why," it helps to have a plan of action—but not too rigid of a plan. Stepping-stone goals (many, many of them) to get you from Point A to Point X are necessary.

Sometimes, the steps you follow won't work out the way you'd hoped. Support yourself by acknowledging and pivoting: "Okay, that sucks, I'm gonna go drown my sorrows in a pepperoni pizza, and then tomorrow I'll adjust my plan of action."

We may not have much control over what happens to us, but we have loads of control over how we handle it. How will you position this rejection in your life? How can you come back from this disappointment? How can you climb out of your rock bottom? By transforming a failure into something learned, you're less likely to take the bad stuff so personally or feel so betrayed by your Muse or by the industry.

Conversely, when you strike a win, how will you celebrate? How will you honor how far you're coming along? Getting excited about small successes is a great way to remind yourself that everything you're doing is about more than reaching your audacious goal. You're growing and learning and becoming a better version of yourself. Be grateful for the stepping-stone wins.

One of the most beautiful things about a writing journey is that it's completely personalized and crafted from scratch. No two journeys are alike, and you can't copy someone else's journey and expect to find success. That's because you're operating with your one-of-a-kind Muse, which is directly tied to your one-of-a-kind natural writing forces. You have a unique creative system at your fingertips that you can put to work in any way that feels good to you.

It's much easier to work alongside this creative system when you've identified yourself as a writer, made a commitment to honor your journey, and understand your "why." Does that mean you won't suffer disappointments or setbacks? No, and it doesn't even mean you're guaranteed the success you crave.

What it does mean is that you'll live and write by standards and values that are authentic to you. That you'll take meaningful actions that earn you wins. That you'll grow from the writer you are now to the writer you want to become.

I know I've said repeatedly that all writing journeys are as unique as the writer, and that to blaze your own trail means depending on your natural writing forces. However, sometimes, it's nice to see an example of what a journey might look like to help you get started.

Below is a sample of a journey that Simone, one of my writing clients, followed:

Dream goal: Sell my MG action-adventure novel to one of the Big Five publishers.

Natural writing forces that benefit me: I'm hard-working, self-motivated, and task-focused. I thrive on positive reinforcement. I have a wonderful support system made up of my husband, parents, two friends from college who are also writers, a local writing group, and a writing coach I hired. I can work on my writing approximately 1.5 hours without disruptions every night, five nights a week.

Natural writing forces that hinder me: I have a hard time saying "no" to invitations to go out with friends, knowing I'll miss a writing session. I revise while writing because I'm a perfectionist. I compare myself to writers I follow on social media and tell myself I'll never be as successful as them.

Goal plan: Finish the third draft of my book by the end of the year. Write 5 nights a week for a minimum of 1.5 hours each night. (Taking the month of May off because of family vacation, including a wedding.) In July, I'll start sending pages to my writing coach for her feedback. Read and study at least 5 MG action-adventure novels that have been traditionally published in the past three years. I'll return to a regular blogging schedule no later than June. (Still need to put this into a physical calendar for stronger accountability!!!)

Other tasks: Learn how to write a query letter and a synopsis. Write a list of ten positive statements and stick it to my computer; get in the habit of repeating them every time I take a writing break.

Rewards: Treat myself to a spa weekend when I finish my draft. For every "No" I tell my friends, I'll put $20.00 in the Fun Jar to save up for a new pair of Jimmy Choos.

When things don't go well, I'll: Take a day off from the novel and spend time at the beach. I'll bring along my journal so I can reflect on how I'm feeling, and then I'll call Nadine (if she's not around, then George) and see if she can get together for coffee and a chat.

As you can see, Simone is a writer who's been entrenched in the writing gig for a while because she's working on the third draft of her novel. She's pinpointed some personality traits and habits that she can use to her benefit, and she's highly aware of how she gets in her own way. She set rewards for herself instead of punishments because she's motivated by positive reinforcement.

You can organize something similar, but be sure to align it with who you are as a writer and who you want to become. For example, Simone didn't include anything about her habitat—the place where she does her writing. She also didn't explore her writing process in detail, or how many words or pages she'd like to target. Simone's map is fairly general; she doesn't provide a monthly or daily writing plan.

We don't know why she doesn't include these things, but it doesn't matter. This is how Simone works, and it's not going to be the same way for anyone else. You may be someone who needs to plan word count targets or outline what an average day looks like—so you must design a map that suits your specific needs and goals.

Here's a sample of a journey that Craig, another past client, followed:

Stepping stone goal: To finish a draft of a novel.

Current struggle: I'm constantly giving up midway through my stories. I have over twenty unfinished stories in a stupid box in my closet, and this makes me disappointed with myself. Right now, I don't care if the story is any good. I just want to finish one for once.

Dream goal: I want to self-publish science fiction stories, but I've got to finish my drafts first!

Word count target: 70,000 words. The most I've ever written is 30K words for a NaNoWriMo story. 70K feels like enough words to make a solid rough draft. I don't care about quality right now. I'll consider the draft finished once I write 70,000 words.

Writing session breakdown: Write for 60 minutes on Monday and Tuesday mornings (7:00–8:00 a.m.) and 60 minutes on Saturday and Sunday afternoons (1:00–2:00 p.m.). My word count target each week is 2,000 words.

Workspace: I set up a table in my basement with good lighting. I have everything I need to work down there, and my partner agreed to leave me alone during this time.

Accountability: Meet with my writing group online every other Thursday evening at 6:30 p.m. I'm not sending pages, but I'll talk about my progress. Journal self-assessments every Sunday night.

Natural writing forces that benefit me: My support system that includes my partner and my writing group, my workspace that is conducive to writing, my schedule to write.

Red flags: Negative self-talk and rewriting scenes. I compare my rough work with published work.

Solution(s): I'm staying off social media for this period of time to avoid comparison-itis.

Reward: Once I reach 70K words, my partner promised me a weekend at our favorite getaway.

This is an example of a stepping-stone goal that Craig needs to accomplish before he can move toward his dream goal. He's plagued by an inability to finish his stories, so he decided to remove the pressure of "quality" and focus on overcoming a major obstacle.

His hope is that when he can finish a draft (just based on word count), that he'll prove to himself he's a finisher, and he'll be able to make forward progress in his overall journey.

If you decide to map your next writing journey, please remember this is merely a path of guiding lights. It's not the end-all and be-all of anything. And if something unexpected happens, it's important to remain open-minded and flexible. You can't account for every possible twist and turn, nor should you! Part of creativity is learning how to adjust, how to see silver linings to clouds, and how to turn a setback into an opportunity.

You're already the hero of your own story. The journey you follow is up to you.

DISCOVERY WORK

Get yourself a blank sheet of paper and some pens, colored pencils, or markers. In the center, write down a major goal you want to accomplish and circle it. This could be your Audacious Dream, or it could be something that feels more within reach. For the purposes of this exercise, we'll refer to this goal as Point X, but for your purposes, concretely and specifically describe this goal on your sheet of paper.

Draw a line from that circle and write down a stepping-stone task that you'd need to accomplish to help you get to Point X. Don't worry yet where this stepping-stone task is situated in the line-up of other stepping-stone tasks. You're just doing some imagining right now.

Repeat this process of drawing a line from Point X and writing down a stepping-stone task until you feel satisfied. It might look cramped and messy. That's okay.

Now, take another sheet of paper and start assessing the order of your stepping-stone tasks. Which one would you logically do today or tomorrow? This is considered Point A of your journey. If you don't have one that makes sense, leave it blank for now, but make sure you return to it. You want to give yourself an immediate task, no matter how small or insignificant it may seem.

Decide what other tasks could be carried out in the short term, either in the next couple of days or within a week or two. Again, if you don't have anything that feels plausible, leave this for now, but come back later to make sure you're plugging in tasks where they'd serve you best.

Next, ask yourself what tasks you'd accomplish by the end of the next 30 days? Sixty days? Ninety days? Six months? A year? Longer?

You probably see where I'm going with this. You're creating a practical schedule based on your mind map. This schedule can be as flexible and broad as you want it to be, or you can get super-specific with tasks down to the hour. Do what feels good to you.

I recommend reverse-engineering once you have a line-up in place. Working backwards, from Point X to Point A will help you see things from a different perspective, and you might realize you overlooked or forgot a step.

When you can fill in all possible tasks and necessary timelines (these will depend on Point X and where you're at presently in relation to the goal), then you've set stepping stones that will eventually lead you to your destination.

At this point, you can ask yourself if you're willing to spend the next year or three years or whatever on your journey. Decide on an end-date and mark it on a calendar or in your journal. Or, maybe you want to keep things open-ended—totally cool. You can always schedule a "creative health check-up" at any point in your journey to assess how you're feeling about things, and change your mind as needed.

Mapping out a potential route to Point X will help you see what you need to do over the short and long term. It also will give you a sense of control about how this journey impacts you emotionally, psychologically, and mentally. Regular creative health check-ups and a willingness to pivot and try something different are other helpful strategies that can aid any decisions you have to make.

33

BELIEVE IN YOUR AUDACIOUS DREAM

We all have dreams. Some are more audacious than others. It's the audacious ones that seem to trip us up, even though they're the ones we want the most. An Audacious Dream can ironically make us play small—we start thinking we're not cut out for it, and the self-sabotaging begins.

Audacious Dreams aren't impossible to reach. However, our limiting beliefs make us feel unworthy. Our perception of our circumstances creates our experiences.

If we believe we have no time, we have no time.

If we believe we can't finish a story, we can't finish a story.

If we believe we can't reach our goals, we can't reach our goals.

We prepare our environment for the outcome we expect.

It's like what we might do when we have company visiting. We clean our house, put out the fancy guest towels, buy the better snacks—all because we want to provide the best experience for our company. We want them to enjoy their stay with us.

We do what we *need* to do in order to accomplish what we *want* to do. But if we attach limits on what we want to do by telling ourselves *we can't* or *we shouldn't*, then we have effectively narrowed our options and our opportunities.

We will act out what we believe is possible.

If we believe we can't, then we won't.

The good news, though, is that if we believe we can, then we *will.*

That's under your control—through your natural writing forces.

One of the questions I wanted you to ask yourself in the chapter on natural writing forces concerns what you believe about your writing journey. What did you write down? Take a minute to mull that over. Is it empowering or limiting? Can you expound on that? What do you believe about who you are as a writer? What do you believe is possible for you, as a writer?

When I run mindset coaching sessions with my writing clients, a huge part of our work involves identifying their limiting beliefs and then reframing them into empowering beliefs about themselves, their Muse, and their writing journey.

The reason we do this work is to help us stay out of our own way as we strive to reach our Audacious Dreams. Writing is hard enough, y'all, without adding our gremlins to the mix.

I'm not saying you'll defeat every last gremlin that preys upon you—otherwise, you'd be perfect, and there's no such thing as perfect. However, what I am saying is that by doing this work, you'll build a particular set of skills that will aid you in your journey forth, enabling you to build a strong and healthy relationship with your Muse.

Some beliefs that work to your benefit:

- You must believe that creativity is your birthright.

- You must honor your desire to create.

- When creating brings you joy, then you're bringing joy into your life and the lives of others.

- Your creativity contributes to your emotional, spiritual, mental, and physical health.

- Pursuing a creative life that fulfills you is living in your truth.

I realize how hard it can be to get from "I'm not a good writer" to anything close to what's listed above, but a flourishing writing practice comes from a flourishing mindset. It's important to seed empowering beliefs into your daily self-talk so that they become a natural part of your internal landscape.

You're probably going to guess what I'm about to say next: Journal this stuff through! Pay attention to what thoughts and feelings (and beliefs!) come up for you. Jot down as much as you can because all of this makes up your current state of being. Anything negative or critical can be reframed into positive and supportive. It's never too early—or too late—to flip your self-talk around so that you're treating yourself with confidence, love, and empowered beliefs.

A final word—

Stories are as unique, individual, and special as the writer crafting them. All stories have structure, personality, and heart. Finding those key pieces requires determination and ferocity to endure the long game of story development and a strong devotion to your Muse.

Writing a story is a personal endeavor, even when you're writing for an audience. The journey you choose to forge should be grounded in the kind of writer you want to be. Your path completely hinges on your global vision, the choices you make to attain that vision, and the motivation behind your choices.

You can learn basic writing skills and fundamental storytelling concepts through the guidance of other writers or teachers. Constructing and refining a story can also be learned via workshops, one-on-one coaching, or group feedback.

But what needs to come directly from you, from the heart of you, is the specific story you want to tell and how you want to tell it. This will involve originality and your personal creative expression, which can only be learned by doing the work and having a solid grasp of your personal strengths, processes, and goals.

Get comfortable with the natural writing forces that serve you because that's your operating system. It's what will launch you, and it's what will sustain you—but only if you know how to read the manual!

And for those forces that hinder you, learn how to tame them or do the work to uproot them.

When things feel insurmountable, it's easy to turn against yourself, but I encourage you to be your own best teammate. And remember, no matter what, your Muse will always be there for you, ready to create whenever you say the word.

Ready to help you become the writer you want to be.

DISCOVERY WORK

Are you ready to upgrade your writing life? Do you wish to be a better version of the writer you are today? What would your creative life look like if you already have what you want? How would you feel? How would you behave? What actions would you take? What would be your beneficial habits?

When you know who you want to become as a writer, then it's much easier to figure out what you need to change about your current creative lifestyle to become that new version.

Step 1.| Start by visualizing this new version of you living your ideal writing life. If you can, meditate on this version for a few minutes, and then jot down everything you remember in a journal. Be sure to explain why this version is important to you and how this upgrade is different from the life you're currently living.

Step 2.| The extent to which you don't have the writing life you desire is the extent to which you're resisting it on some level. You might be fearful of what it'll take to reach this milestone, or you may feel like you aren't worthy of such a win.

Assessing your current writing lifestyle, your worldview, and your natural writing forces is a great way to figure out what isn't quite working so you can make concrete shifts today that will positively influence your journey.

Below are some questions to get you started:

1.| What have I been avoiding or resisting?
2.| What is my overall emotion when it comes to my writing life?
3.| Who is on my team? Who can I depend on?
4.| Is my writing workspace in the best possible shape to help me succeed?
5.| Do I use my time efficiently for maximum output?
6.| Am I overwhelmed because I haven't set proper boundaries?
7.| Could I set stronger deadlines to help me combat procrastination?
8.| What kinds of rewards (or penalties) would motivate me?
9.| Which natural writing forces work against me?
10.| Which natural writing forces serve me?
11.| What do I not know about my situation?

[For all of these questions, be sure you're following up with *Why* or *Why not?* Understanding the motivation behind your actions or attitude will help you accurately diagnose how you're holding yourself back.]

Step 3.| Once you're clear on what isn't quite working in your current writing life, take another look at the notes you journaled about the writer you want to be. Meditate on that visualization again because I want you to take it one step further by thinking *as if* . . .

This is an imagination game you can play every day that helps to form empowering beliefs around your visualization of the writing life you want. Basically, you'll write a whole story around your visualization, and when you tap into this story on a daily basis, it'll become easier and easier to believe your dream is possible.

Not only do you want to see this new version and new lifestyle in your mind's eye, you want to feel *as if* it's really happening. When you tie positive, anticipatory emotions to this vision, you'll begin to reframe your belief system, shifting out of doubt and into possibility.

Complete the following prompts from the perspective of the writer you want to become. Modify any of the prompts as you see fit and add your own!

1.| As a published author, I'm best known for . . .

2.| When I reached one of my writing goals, I made this exciting shift in my life . . .

3.| As a published author, my typical day looks like . . .

4.| This celebrity invited me to dinner because they loved my book so much . . .

5.| The next project I'm psyched to begin is . . .

6.| My success in my writing life has allowed me to . . .

7.| One of the best lessons I've learned that has helped me rise to success is . . .

8.| I'm grateful for these three things . . .

9.| In the next three months, I'd like to accomplish . . .

10.| In the next year, I'd like to accomplish . . .

ACKNOWLEDGEMENTS

My original vision for this book was to write a guide that could help another writer start, develop, and even finish a draft to a story. As this project blossomed and evolved, and I edged ever closer to wrapping it up and sending it on to my editor, things got real. I choked. Put the book on hold. Sat on it for weeks here, days there. When I was feeling some confidence, I'd pick through it, maybe write a brand-new chapter, or maybe I'd scrap twenty pages. Then I'd put it away again.

I struggled to understand what my nerves were all about. I've taught all this stuff before. I've been a story coach for many years. What's the big deal?

Then I realized what was holding me back: Deep down, I worried that my book wasn't good enough. Even though I've used all these techniques and discovery questions and strategies in my own writing journey and shared them with clients, my inner critic, Eris, snubbed this project at every turn.

I had to find a way to overcome my fears, or else this book would never see the light of day. As a result, I'm not the same writer at the end of this project as I was when I started. Ironically, that's a large part of what this book teaches. Holy cats, it's a wild feeling, knowing that the mere undertaking of this project helped me learn something new about myself, conquer self-doubt, and push onward to accomplish a goal.

Once I decided that I was going to finish this book and publish it, no matter what, I was able to seek the support of people I knew would hold me upright through it all. Without them, I would still be sitting on this book, drumming up excuse after excuse about why I can't work on it.

First, my husband and children. Each of you is a rock I can lean on when the going gets tough and when I let my self-criticism get the best of me. Y'all have given me the space and time I've requested so that I can pursue my dreams of writing, and I know that it wasn't always easy—especially when dinner was late to the table, or I was hunkered down in my study for hours upon hours trying to beat deadlines. I have the best family in the world—I love y'all more than pizza.

Second, Alison Huff, who I met through an online writing group, and who is, hands down, the best editor I have ever worked with. Alison's eye for detail, knowledge of fiction writing and the editing process, and her marvelously positive (and funny!) comments throughout the book kept me moving in a forward direction. Alison also pitched in to format the book in the final stages, getting this project over some major bumps in the road and saving my sanity. Thank you so much, Alison! You took this book to the next level, and I'm so grateful for your help, generosity, and friendship.

I honestly don't know what I would have done without you along for the ride.

I also want to thank Tom Holbrook for the cover design, formatting, and for being on hand to answer my questions about the publishing process. Tom's knowledge and expertise gave me the boost I needed to (finally) wrap up the final draft and move on to the next phase—publishing and marketing. Thanks, Tom!

Finally, to all my Team Writer members, Museletter subscribers, writing colleagues, and writing clients—you're marvelous. I'm grateful that you've chosen to spend time learning from me, writing alongside me, following my blog, or reading one of my Museletters. There are a lot of writing coaches in the world, and the fact you sometimes hang out in my little nook in the Cosmos is an absolute delight and honor. Thank you for being a part of my community and thank you for helping me grow as a writer and a writing coach.

REFERENCES

Chapter 1:

Muse definition:
Merriam-Webster, s.v. "app (n.)," accessed July 26, 2024,
merriam-webster.com/dictionary/app
Maya Angelou - mayaangelou.com

Chapter 2:

Statistic National Library of Medicine, Prevalence, Predictors, and Treatment of Impostor Syndrome: a Systematic Review, published online Dec. 17, 2019 ncbi.nlm.nih.gov/pmc/articles/PMC7174434

Chapter 4:

Gabby Bernstein - gabbybernstein.com
Shakti Gawain - shakti-gawain.com

Chapter 10:

Save the Cat - savethecat.com

Chapter 17:

Maslow, A.H. (1943). A theory of human motivation. Psychological Review, 50(4), 370-396. doi.org/10.1037/h0054346

AUTHOR'S NOTE

Thank you so much for your purchase of *You and Your Muse*. Did you know that you just helped me support endangered species across the planet through my fundraising program, Writers for Wildlife?

To learn more, check out Writers for Wildlife: katejohnstonauthor.com/writers-for-wildlife

I hope you enjoyed this book. If so, would you consider rating and reviewing *You and Your Muse* on Amazon.com or any other book review platform? Leaving reviews helps authors like me (and like you!) build an audience that benefits from their work.

This book is only a small nugget of my products and services I offer to writers. If you're interested in learning more from me, please join my Museletter community at katejohnstonauthor.com to receive monthly letters containing tips and strategies, updates on new books, plus exclusive invitations to writer chats where you can get the support and guidance you need to move forward on your writing journey.

ABOUT THE AUTHOR

Kate Johnston is a writing and mindset coach, editor, and author. Her clients range from budding writers to traditionally published authors. Writers hire her to guide them through the story development process and mindset gremlins so they can transform their dreams of writing a book into reality. When not writing or working with writers, Kate spends her time with the fairies in her garden, reading a good book, watching a Disney movie, or hanging out with her family and friends.

Instagram: instagram.com/katejauthor
Writing group: facebook.com/groups/TeamWriter
Website: katejohnstonauthor.com
Pinterest: pinterest.com/katejauthor

www.ingramcontent.com/pod-product-compliance
Lightning Source LLC
Chambersburg PA
CBHW030910120626
46554CB00001B/81